W9-DAN-772

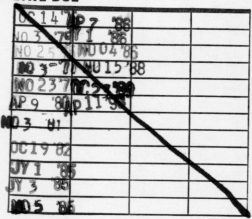

Administering Federalism in a Democracy

PUBLIC ADMINISTRATION AND DEMOCRACY

SERIES EDITOR   ROSCOE C. MARTIN

PUBLISHED

FREDERICK C. MOSHER
Democracy and the Public Service

EMMETTE S. REDFORD
Democracy in the Administrative State

OTHER VOLUMES ARE IN PREPARATION

Administering Federalism in a Democracy

ARTHUR W. MACMAHON
Eaton Professor Emeritus of Public Administration
Columbia University

New York
Oxford University Press
1972

Preface

THE LITERATURE OF FEDERALISM has dealt little with its administrative side. The prevailing concerns have been constitutional and legal, though with attention also to history and politics. A main question has been the partitioning of legislative powers. It would be mistaken as well as idle to quarrel with these tendencies in themselves. Federalism is a legal contrivance. This feature is a phase of its importance as one of mankind's inventions. Part of its virtue as a way of combining the one and the many lies in its constitutional framework and the crucial role played by the courts. To disregard these aspects of federalism would be to obscure and belittle the subject. This book takes account of these aspects, although its special concern is the way federalism is administered in the United States.

Federalism in the modern world is in no wise uniform in either form or practice, for there are many variations among the dozen constitutions that call themselves federal. Moreover, change is frequent, even continuous. In particular, significant changes have marked the development of federalism in the United States, especially, one is tempted to say, in recent years. They involve more than quickened attention to long-established features. In addition is the swift and mounting accumulation of administrative relations, both vertical and horizontal, among governments at all levels, that are so varied, in the mass so extensive, and so promising in their tendencies that it is not too much to speak of a change in the nature of federalism. These developments in the United States and elsewhere in the world invite a study of federal administration and justify the writing of this book.

Poughkeepsie, N. Y.   *A. W. M.*
Summer 1971

Foreword

THE AUTHOR OF THIS BOOK, Arthur W. Macmahon, for many years has ranked in the forefront of American students of public affairs. He is the author of many works centering on (but in no wise limited to) public administration. His best-known book may be *Federalism Mature and Emergent,* a notable collection of essays which he arranged and edited (and to which he contributed) as one of the Bicentennial Conference Series publications of Columbia University.

Early in his career Professor Macmahon conceived a lively and lasting interest in the fence row which separates, and at the same time joins, democracy and public administration. Some years ago, indeed, as a visiting professor he taught a course by that title at Syracuse University: the course in fact which gave rise to the Oxford University Press series on the subject. It seemed entirely natural, therefore, to make inquiry as to his possible interest in writing a book in the series. Happily Mr. Macmahon was interested. *Administering Federalism in a Democracy* is the result of the author's lifelong interest in the subject.

Those who know Arthur Macmahon would not expect him to write a narrowly professional or specialized book under this (or any other) title. He has in fact not written such a book here, but rather a broad study of federalism whose central concern is nevertheless indicated by his title. If the author has not written a technical analysis of the relation between the federal system and the democratic society, he has produced a study which gives evidence on every page of his sound scholarship and his deep understanding of both federalism and democracy. We are pleased and honored to have him as a contributor to this series on democracy and public administration.

ROSCOE C. MARTIN

Contents

Administering Federalism in a Democracy

I

Federalism as a Constitutional System

FEDERALISM IN MODERN NATIONS is a constitutional form that divides lawmaking powers between a central government for the whole area and a number of constituent governments. The arrangement is legal in essence. The practice is largely administrative. Both features appear variously in the dozen-odd countries that proclaim themselves to be federal. Both are prominent in the relations among the governmental levels that are increasingly important in the United States. In different but converging ways the same trend exists, for example, in the federal systems of continental Europe (notably in Switzerland and in West Germany) where the central government uses the administrative facilities of the member states as its agents. In the recent federations as well as in the older schemes there is an underlying merger of methods.

The federal principle must be distinguished both from the constitutional structure of the unitary governments and from the kinds of union that are called confederal. In the latter cases the central machinery arises out of the member states as governments; it is supported by their financial contributions and acts mainly through them. A confederation is more than an international union because the central decisions do not require a unanimous vote by the spokesmen for the participating countries. Federalism implies an arrangement that is still more organic and is suited for decisive action nationally.

The federal form as a type of political association is fitting where two or more groups differ in language or otherwise, or where a homogeneous people are spread over a large area but share enough interests to act through a central government while the parts are self-governing for important purposes. A critical feature is the partitioning of power under a constitution that cannot be altered legally by the mere passage of a national law. The central government must be sufficiently related to the whole people as citizens so that it has its own basis for action, including the crucial authority to raise money by taxation and the power to regulate certain matters. These characteristics need not bar the central government from using the facilities of the member states and thus acting through them, or from collaborating with them through grants of money or the loan of personnel or other forms of mutual assistance.

Federalism in a loosely figurative meaning of the word covers many arrangements, public and private, where the one and the many are combined in ways that preserve the autonomy of the separate parts. The term must be used more precisely in speaking of governments. The variations are wide, however; much of the interest lies in the inventiveness and especially in the administrative adaptations that are found in the old as well as the new systems. At mid-century slightly more than one-third of the world's population lived in countries that constitutionally proclaimed themselves to be federal. Federalism is therefore widely spread in the world, though in fact less widely than the countries that call themselves federal. "Historically," wrote Crane Brinton, "real federal unions have been relatively few, hard to establish, and limited to groups which already possessed much, and that much positive, not a mere negation like fear, in common."[1]

The outright abandonments of federalism in recent times have not been numerous as distinguished from the ostensible federations that have survived in name but as virtually unitary governments. In the Caribbean the plan to link a number of the larger islands was abandoned before it had been tried fully; in any case it was lacking in needful central powers. In central Africa the determination of the white minority to preserve their hegemony in what is now the independent country of Rhodesia was the reason for the breakup of the federal scheme that had existed for a short time. In the nineteenth century certain regional federations in South America and Central America were given up after longer periods of use. These examples confirm the view that the constitutional essence of federalism is not easy to install nor is it easily maintained over a long, changeful period.

The Case for Federalism

At this point it is appropriate to state the case for a federal structure of government when the reasons for it are more than a minimum necessary in securing some degree of union. First, federalism is a means, in countries where diversity is pronounced, of accommodating government to the consent of the governed. Second, federalism is a device for allowing flexibility where the total area is large. Third, a federal system is likely to make experimentation easier. To be sure, central governments in unitary systems engage in much experimentation, but the existence of a federal system heightens the opportunity and encourages the practice. Fourth, federalism widens the opportunity for participation in government. This results from the existence of legislative bodies in the member states and also from elective executives and their aides.

1. Crane Brinton, *From Many One* (Cambridge, Mass.: Harvard University Press, 1948), p. 105.

Finally, a federal system avoids undue concentration of political power. It tends to decentralize the structure of the political parties. By multiplying the arenas of political decision it increases the likelihood that the minority party of the moment will have footholds in some places with opportunities for the demonstration of executive competence and the maturing of new leadership. Structurally, federalism has a self-fortifying effect. Politically, the existence of the member states guarantees the survival of local influences in party policy quite apart from the formal powers of those states.

A Roster of Federations

Amid the many variants of contemporary federalism, the term must be used more broadly than it was by Kenneth C. Wheare, who found federal systems only in the United States, Canada, Switzerland, and Australia.[2] It is well for us to be more tolerant. The scope of federalism cannot be imprisoned by the meaning it had during the laissez faire period that preceded the social movements and vastly expanded public policies of today.

A roster of existing federal systems shows the need for flexibility as well as care in the use of words. Alexis de Tocqueville was referring particularly to federal arrangements in the United States when he wrote in the thirties of the last century that "the human understanding more easily invents new things than new words. . . ."[3] He was not sure what term to apply to the system he studied in 1830. But the United States helped to fix the word federalism as the name for a mixed form of government. The word must be used within limits, as has been said, but every decade of experience with federal forms shows increasingly the need for a wide-ranging usage. In the United States, after the admis-

2. K. C. Wheare, *Federal Government* (New York: Oxford University Press, 1947).

3. Alexis de Tocqueville, *Democracy in America*, Vol. I, in the Henry Reeve translation as revised by Francis Bowen with an introduction by Phillips Bradley, (New York: Knopf, 1945), p. 158.

sion of Hawaii and Alaska as states, there remained the unique situation of Puerto Rico as a "commonwealth" within the union.

Today Canadian federalism, which drew the provinces together in the middle of the nineteenth century, is revitalized by the restlessness of French-speaking Quebec. In Australia a federal union was finally achieved in 1900, in part by international portents of danger. On the European continent the linkage of the Swiss cantons did indeed have ancient roots. It is well said that the country "is kept together, and kept apart, by history."[4] Federation in West Germany after World War II is more valid than was the case when Prussia, overwhelmingly predominant in the empire, survived in the federal republic after the first great war. Also on the European continent Belgium seeks to apply aspects of the federal idea (calling its version *l'état communitaire*) in arranging a compromise between the French-speaking and the Flemish-speaking parts of the country. In Austria the validity of federalism lies partly in the political and other forces that are dominant in Vienna as against those that are prominent in the more rural parts. In the Middle East a number of areas joined in the Federation of South Arabia.[5] In 1971 a larger, though loose, project was the forming of the Federation of Arab Republics by Egypt, Syria, and Libya.

Of Yugoslavia it could be said that "the federal structure could not be dismissed as window dressing, for it helped to satisfy important psychological needs of the Yugoslav peoples for recognition of their national individuality, and perhaps more important, it gave each nationality the assurance, for the first time, of enjoying a truly equal status with the other national groups."[6] In Czechoslovakia, however, the federal

4. Christopher Hughes, *The Parliament of Switzerland* (London: Cassell, 1962), p. 1.
5. R. L. Watts, *New Federations: Experiments in the Commonwealth* (Oxford: Clarendon Press, 1966), p. 5.
6. Paul Shoup, *Communism and the Yugoslav National Question* (New York: Columbia University Press, 1968), p. 119.

arrangement in 1970 between the Czech and Slovak element was largely nullified by the dictatorial party. Much the same thing must be said of federalism in Russia, although the constitution there says the member states may secede and two of them—the Ukraine and Byelorussia—are allowed to have diplomatic representatives abroad. It can at least be said of the Soviet version of federalism that "one should not underestimate the symbolic satisfaction that the trappings of autonomous 'statehood,' however insubstantial, have given to the ethnic pride of the minorities."[7]

In Asia the constitutional system of India introduced features that are still novel in the practice of federalism. Pakistan's constitutional solution of the relations of its two widely separated parts remains unresolved. In Malaysia, where federalism has grown in part from agreements among chiefs or sultans, the ethnic diversities that exist between the Malay peoples (who comprise about half of the population) and the numerous Chinese are factors that contribute to the vitality of that country's version of federalism even after the withdrawal of Singapore as a member of the union.

In Latin America the federal dream of Bolívar, the liberator, lapsed early in the nineteenth century. The ostensibly federal constitutions of Mexico, Brazil, Argentina, and Venezuela are vitiated in part by the sweeping nature of the conferral of central power, in part by the practice of intervention under their constitutions, and in part by military governments in some of the countries.

On the African continent the outstanding federal experiment is in Nigeria, reorganized as twelve member states after the unsuccessful secession effort of one of the regions. As things have gone generally in Africa the nascent spirit of nationalism has led to many separate and often small countries. Thus far more is heard of independence than of any wide need for federal association.

7. Erich Goldhagen (ed.), *Ethnic Minorities in the Soviet Union* (New York: Praeger, 1968), p. ix.

Basic Constitutional Features

With the foregoing variants among existing systems in view, it is timely to restate the basic features of a federal scheme of government. First, the constitutional division of power between the central and the constituent governments cannot be changed by ordinary legislation, but can be modified only through a special amending process. The fundamental importance attached to constitutional law points to a judiciary that will act as an umpire, interpreting and applying the constitution and passing upon the constitutionality of the enactments and actions of the central government as well as those of the constituent governments.

Second, the powers of the constituent governments in a federation must be considerable, not trivial. This feature, however, is relative and debatable. The meaning of what is important varies among countries and changes through time. In general the tendencies at work in the modern world draw an increasing array of policies to the centers of federal systems, at least for prime decisions, although their execution and enlargement may remain largely in the hands of the member states or localities within them.

A third feature of federalism is the legal equality of the member states of the union. Historically the underlying idea of legal equality was a major contribution of the United States to the theory of federalism. This principle is not inconsistent with the wide variation among the member states in geographical size, population, and resources. It remains true, as John Stuart Mill argued in his notable comments on federalism, that no individual member state should be so powerful that it could rely upon its individual strength in protecting itself against attack.

Fourth, each member state must have not only a fairly complete government but also wide scope in deciding on its form and procedures. In practice there has been less originality and less diversity in the forms of government than in

theory is open to the member states. In the United States, for
example, the individual states have had more freedom under
the constitution to vary their forms of government than they
have chosen to exercise. Thus no apparent reason exists in
theory why some or all of them might not have turned from
the national model of a "presidential system" to a parliamentary form of government. Further, only one state (Nebraska)
has adopted a unicameral legislature, a form obviously available to all.

Clashes among the different geographical sections of a
country about fundamental social institutions may risk a dis-
ruption. It is still to be shown, for example, that a federation
as such would survive for a long time in a country where different member states were dominated separately by communist
and non-communist regimes, each pursuing its policy in a
vigorous way. In India the test of this issue has been avoided
in part through the intervention of the central government
under the emergency clauses of the national constitution.

In the different case of the United States the institution of
slavery was a source of disunion from the outset. The constitutional draftsmen of 1787 were aware of the hazards of a geographical schism, especially in view of the increasingly sectional distribution of slavery. James Madison as a Convention
member (according to notes made by Yates, a fellow member)
said: "The great danger for our general government is that
the southern and northern interests of the continent are opposed to each other, not from their differences of size, but
from climate, and principally from the effect of their having
or not having slaves." And, in developing further his point
that the main difference did not lie between large and small
states on grounds of size in itself, he added (referring to the
legislative body under the Articles of Confederation): "Look
to the votes in Congress; most of them stand divided by the
geography of the country, not by the size." The clash in the
Convention was muffled by compromises in the original constitution. A final break was avoided for more than sixty years.

Meanwhile the country increased in population and in national consciousness. There also grew (offsetting the profitability of cotton as an export crop that was helped by the invention of the cotton gin at home and the development of machinery abroad) a deepening moral indignation about slavery. When, in the face of a permanently minority position in the growing country, eleven southern states attempted to secede, the rupture of the federal union was prevented by four years of civil war. It was followed by social changes and constitutional amendments that were profound in part, although limited in their actual effects through most of the following century.

In retrospect one hesitates to call the American Civil War inevitable even when he assumes that slavery had to stop; perhaps an indemnity might have secured emancipation without war. Nevertheless the crisis in federalism in the United States a century ago is at least a warning about the type of issue that may challenge the comity of a federal system. It was more glaring as a lesson than the seven weeks' Swiss War of the Sonderbund (also in the middle of the nineteenth century) that prevented the secession of the Catholic cantons. That revolt was quickly crushed and Switzerland survived as a federation of two religions and three languages.

In the federal system of the United States and Australia, notably, the early diversities were rooted in separate settlements along an extended sea coast. They survived partly in occupying a large and physically varied continent. In both cases, the enduring diversities were in the land itself. These influences were heightened in the United States by factors that included the sectional survival of slavery and the tragic aftermath of its consequences as seen in cities generally. Basically, however, the spatial factors are dominant in explaining the variations that exist in a country with one language and with a self-canceling multiplicity of church affiliations.

In the part of North America that became the United States, people were on the move always. Today this stirring about is increasing. But there has been a difference between the kind of movements (straining the adjectives) that can be called molar and the kind today that is molecular. The movement of people in the United States today mainly involves individuals and families. In contrast, especially during the period that is remembered in American history as the western movement, people shifted often in groups. Villages in some newly opened areas, for example, often took on some of the appearance and some of the reality of New England towns. A later and permanent change came in the twentieth century. Previously, from 1850 to 1900, each decennial census showed a larger proportion of the people living at census time in the state in which they had been born. It was this trend (destined to change after 1900) that led Frederick Jackson Turner to write in 1908: "I make the suggestion that as the nation reaches a more stable equilibrium, with denser population pressing upon the means of existence, with the population no longer migratory, the influence of the diverse physiographic provinces which make up the nation will become more marked." The author wrote against the background of the fact that the 1900 census had shown 79.1 per cent of the people living in the state of their birth as compared with 75.8 per cent in 1850. Turner did not foresee what was revealed by the 1910 census: that the percentage of individuals living at census time in the state of their birth had again begun to drop. Nowadays it is mainly a movement of individuals and their families; it is no longer "molar" in the sense that describes much of the movement during the earlier part of the preceding century. A present exception has been the widespread movement of blacks to northern cities.

The boundaries of the constituent states within a federal system become fixed usually before the future patterns of life are fully revealed; the long-run outcome is likely to be uncertain always. Indeed in the United States the divisions among the original colonies along the seaboard were shaped by circumstances that were mainly demographic, although distorted in part by the accidents of royal favoritism. Later, in carving the western territory into states, knowledge was scanty about the topography, not to mention the understandable lack of knowledge about the probable distribution of people in the long-run and the nature of the industries that would develop and change through time. It is true that in the period before the Civil War some attention was given in Congress to the possible ways in which the number and the conformation of the newly admitted states might affect the relative strength of the slave-owning and the non-slave-owning parts of the country. Mostly, however, it was convenient to define the areas of the new states either in terms of lines of latitude and longitude or to use sizable rivers as the most visible feature in a terrain that often was incompletely explored.

The use of rivers as boundaries overlooked the fact that navigable streams tend to invite a common culture and interchange on both banks. Only temporarily in the United States, when water transport languished and before bridges multiplied, did the unifying role of rivers lessen for a time. The emerging situation is shown in the fact that twenty-three of the so-called standard metropolitan areas cross state boundaries. Much traffic that is local in fact becomes interstate commerce. A geographer, C. B. Fawcett, who wrote about frontiers among other matters, remarked: "In the vast majority of cases the drawbacks of a river boundary for a civilized stage in a settled and populous land far outweigh the advantage of its easy recognition."

An exception in the United States was the well-conceived boundary between New York State and the New England settlements. It runs on high land about twenty miles east of the Hudson River. This line was established by treaty while the Dutch still had New Amsterdam, later New York City. The boundary line was continued when England acquired the Dutch possessions. Another nearly unique example of a realistic boundary, wisely avoiding the use of a river as the line, has been the line between Massachusetts and New Hampshire. It follows the Merrimac River but at a distance of ten miles north of it. The fortunate result was the fact that the manufacturing towns along the stream, with some of the factories bestriding it, are not directly involved in interstate commerce.

In contrast with these mainly exceptional examples, rivers are widely used as interstate boundaries in the United States. As a result, many of the country's largest cities, rising naturally on the rivers and helped further by the railroads along their banks, are located at the edges of the states. Local traffic is turned automatically into interstate commerce.

To mention these facts, however, is not to quarrel with the outcome of history. Stability for the boundaries of the areas in a federation has important advantages. It is true that some adjustments may be useful in the early stages of the federalizing process. The shifts may include some readjustments of boundaries that involve an increase in the number of states. In India, for example, these developments have resulted in part from the restlessness of certain areas on religious and like grounds. It has been noted that Nigeria, struggling to find a way amid the tribal and religious, increased the number of member states from four to five and later to a dozen. Doubtless a period of readjustments of the areas is desirable during the early life of federations such as those that have been mentioned. But later geographical shifts (unless minor) are not helpful in matured federations.

In federal systems generally any recasting of state areas, when firmly shaped, is likely to present a dilemma that in itself is a reason for going along with a stabilized pattern. The dilemma involves a conflict between two ideals. One scheme would seek to enhance the role of the future states as homogeneous areas suited for self-expression. It would be likely to result in many states, some of them city-states. The rural areas would be organized separately. The reconstituted states would be uneven in needs and in financial resources. This condition would increase the necessity for support from the national government. Yet such a reshaping of the pattern would be consistent with the argument for federalism as a system that provides for the separate expression of local viewpoints. The other main alternatives in an imagined recasting of state areas would be a system of great provinces, bigger and more varied internally than the existing states. Each would be composite; each would embrace urban and rural areas and a wide diversity of resources and industries. The result would increase the fiscal basis of each part; it would increase the level of self-support of each region. The mixture of elements, however, would make the reshaped areas even less suited than the present states, in a country like the United States, for a coherent kind of self-expression through politics in each state. The dilemma that has just been stated is a cogent reason for going along with the state areas as they exist in a matured federalism such as exists in the United States. It preserves the states as partly self-governing entities but with heavy dependence upon the taxable resources that are available to the country as a whole.

Other Essential Features in a Durable Union

In the circumstances of today's world, a federation must be so arranged and so endowed with powers and restraints that it avoids a number of difficulties that otherwise would weaken and perhaps destroy it unless, as the more probable outcome, they caused it to lose its federal essence in fact, if not in name and form. The hazards to be surmounted may be summarized under five heads. First, the central government may not have enough power to handle the needs that beset it in carrying on the tasks of economic and social planning, conducting the necessary controls, and handling foreign affairs. In the field of international affairs, for example, it can be said that the "real obstacle in the conduct of federal foreign relations seems to be a tenacious localism, which sometimes has its roots grounded in racial prejudice, state patriotism, or selfish provincialism, and which does not

respond to the urgings of international fairness and consistency."[8] The solution to the main problem lies in treating
federations internationally as unitary states.

Second among the difficulties to be overcome is the risk
that the areas of the member states may not be suited to deal
with widespread economic and other problems. A third risk
is the temptation of the member states to set up trade barriers or otherwise to block unduly the movement of persons
and goods throughout the nation, at the cost of weakening
the economy and undermining the basis of freedom. A
fourth source of weakness may be the failure of the central
government to possess and use its fiscal and other influences
in ways that correct the localized deficiencies and that contribute to national development. A fifth difficulty resides
in the fact that social diversities in any society are seldom
distributed geographically in a neat way. Minorities exist at
random. Their needs are partly safeguarded by national
parties in the federation as a whole. Many important rights,
however, must be assured through constitutional guarantees
supported by national courts. Fortunately the existence of
such safeguards is not inconsistent with federalism itself.

Federal constitutions usually give certain powers to the
central government and leave the rest to the constituent governments, subject to such limits as they fix in their own constitutions. But the spirit of federalism is not lost when the
arrangement is reversed. Three instances of the latter pattern
may be noted. The Canadian constitution of 1867 invested
the central government with all unstated powers. In the
Canadian case the reality of this arrangement was soon reversed by judicial interpretations, especially by the breadth
that was given to the concept of "civil affairs" as one of the
powers assigned to the provinces. Apart from Canada, two
constitutions of recent date—those of India and of Nigeria—
enumerate the powers of the constituent states; they also list

8. Harold W. Stoke, *The Foreign Relations of the Federal State* (Baltimore:
The Johns Hopkins Press, 1931), p. 231.

certain central powers (and some concurrent ones as well), but they reserve all unstated matters for central control. This reversal of a pattern for federations that was originally set by the United States is not without significance; it betokens a growing recognition of the policy-shaping responsibilities of the central government in a federation.

THE NEED FOR AN UMPIRE AND FOR GUARANTEES

Two questions arise in preserving the constitutional partitioning of power under federalism. The first and more basic of these issues concerns the nature and location of an umpire that will safeguard the status of the constituent governments while assuring the supremacy of the central government in the fields of responsibility given to it by the constitution, Linked to it is the existence of the guarantees that protect certain basic rights of individuals and groups. The second question is the desirability of providing expressly in the central constitution for some form of national intervention during an emergency in one or more of the constituent areas. These questions must be looked at in turn.

The need for an umpire of some sort is fundamental in the partitioning of legislative powers between the central and the member governments in a federation. From the standpoint of survival the crucial need is to protect the supremacy of the central government. Former Supreme Court Justice Oliver Wendell Holmes remarked that a federal union would doubtless survive as a going system even if the courts did not have the right to invalidate national laws but would not work without the power to invalidate state laws and actions. The courts' power should work both ways. In recent decades, however, the Supreme Court, while invalidating many actions as inconsistent with national legislation or in conflict with constitutional guarantees, has been reluctant to strike down any congressional law of an economic nature. The judiciary has drawn a line between the fundamental personal liberties and the regulation of the country's economy.

In the field of national regulatory action the court has confined itself to the kinds of challenge that ask the Congress to be as clear as possible about the purposes of its laws and their intended coverage. The judicial mood is to defer to the lawmaking bodies, including state legislatures, where Congress has not pre-empted a field of governmental control. This outlook assumes that mostly the elected officials are the proper interpreters of the meaning of the constitution and of the majority will as to the needs for governmental action. Along with this doctrine, however, it is important to note the censorship of legislative and administrative action that is retained and actively exercised by the courts. It covers the fields of personal and group rights, including equal access to the facilities of higher education.

Federalism would be unfair to diffused minorities in the absence of judicially enforceable guarantees of individual and group rights. Without them, critics would have reason to disparage the principle of federalism itself. They might prefer to rely on the protection of minority interests through the competitive interplay of national parties in a unitary system of government. Fortunately the federal constitutions stress increasingly the need for nationwide constitutional guarantees that are construed and enforced by the judiciary.

The Role of Courts in Federal Systems

The role of the courts in the federal system of the United States has been crucial to maintaining the system itself. Their selective action is part of an evolving policy; otherwise the judiciary's decisive power would be inconsistent with democracy itself. The swings of the Supreme Court have been a phase of the country's history which in turn is the story of a people's experience. As recently as 1937, when President Franklin Roosevelt was complaining about the Supreme Court's invalidation of some of the New Deal's enactments and was proposing the corrective popularly called "packing" the court, Senator Carter Glass of Virginia in a nationwide broadcast called on the people, and especially the people of the South, to stand by the Supreme Court that in the past had preserved the position of people of white color. Behind his appeal was a long story of judicial accommodations that had reconciled the practice of many kinds of segregation with the guarantees that were added to the constitution after the Civil War. The occasion of the senator's address was truly a turning point; for it was on that day that the Supreme Court, reversing its decision of the previous year that had invalidated a state minimum wage law, upheld a similar law of another state. It expressly disavowed its previous stand. The court's new ruling was made possible by a shift of one of its members. Fundamentally, however, the constitutional law of the United States had crossed (perhaps forever) a momentous watershed to the other side of doctrine.

The durability of the courts' power in questions of constitutionality lies partly in the extent to which such issues are decided incidentally to the handling of controversies between litigants. It is true that some state constitutions empower the courts of those states to render advisory opinions on the constitutionality of proposed or recent legislation. Moreover, increasing attention is being given nationally to the possibility of lawsuits that may be brought in the name of groups of people. Basically, however, the distinctive quality of the judicial review of legislation in the United States lies, on the one side, in the latent quality and the flexibility of a brief constitution with broad guarantees and, on the other side, in the fact that judicial rulings are made in particular cases after the laws are passed and are being administered. It is true that this arrangement, with its chance reliance upon "test" cases, has weaknesses as well as resilience.[9] Some of the most important developments in domestic as

9. Joel B. Grossman and Joseph Tanenhaus (eds.), *Frontiers of Judicial Research* (New York: Wiley, 1969), p. 423.

well as in foreign policy have never been passed upon in the courts. This fact, however, does not diminish the role played by the courts as umpire in maintaining a reasonable balance in the federal system. Both Congress and (increasingly) administrative agencies have important umpire parts to play, but that of the judiciary is paramount.

The Guarantees of Civil and Other Rights

Experience has confirmed the usefulness of a "bill of rights" in federal constitutions. In the United States twelve proposed amendments to the constitution were submitted by the very first Congress as part of the understanding that had helped to secure ratification by the states. Of these, ten were ratified. Thomas Jefferson, in a letter to Madison shortly after the constitutional convention, had noted certain omissions he did not like in the draft that was awaiting ratification: "a bill of rights, providing clearly, and without the aid of sophism, for freedom of religion, freedom of the press, protection against standing armies, restriction of monopolies, the eternal and unremitting force of the habeas corpus laws, and trials by jury in all matters of fact triable by the laws of the land." In this spirit the First Amendment, adopted in 1791, begins: "Congress shall make no law respecting an establishment of religion, or prohibiting the free exercise thereof, or abridging the freedom of speech, or of the press; or the right of the people peaceably to assemble, and to petition the government for a redress of grievances." The introductory phrase showed that the guarantees were aimed at possible abuses by the national government; this view was accepted by the Supreme Court.

In contrast the amendments that were adopted at the end of the Civil War are to prevent abuses by the state and local governments. Outstanding is the lengthy Fourteenth with its declaration that no state shall "deprive any person of life, liberty, or property, without due process of law; nor deny to any person within its jurisdiction the equal protection of the laws." During recent decades the constitutional doctrines that have amounted almost to a revolution have interfused the First and the Fourteenth Amendments in ways that apply their guarantees both to the central government and to the states and localities. Similarly the Fourteenth has been the basis for making applicable to the states the Fifth Amendment's guarantee of the privilege against self-incrimination.[10]

Other Controls

It is enough to speak briefly of the other kind of control that has been mentioned: non-judicial action by the central government which temporarily displaces the government in one or more constituent states. In retrospect it is obvious that the United States constitution erred by its silence in failing to be explicit about certain features of the federal union. Modern constitutions are usually more exact as to the nature of the union. But very different is the provision in some federal constitutions for intervention by the central government. In Latin American federations this right is conferred and has been used at times in ways that became a negation of the federal principle itself. (We are speaking of action under color of the central constitution itself, not of instances of dictatorship.) Defining the conditions and methods of central intervention, if such permission is given at all, remains one of federalism's most troublesome problems. India's constitution seeks to provide an orderly basis. Nevertheless its use became frequent enough to verge on a negation of the federal idea. Speaking broadly and in the spirit of federalism, the intervention of the central government should be confined to the enforcement of guarantees and obligations under the national constitution and laws that it authorizes, judicially construed and applied.

Examples from Switzerland and Austria show that frequently the auspices for central approval of state action are

10. *Murphy et al. v. Waterfront Commission of New York Harbor,* 378 U.S. 52 (1964).

administrative. The Swiss Federal Council passes upon the legitimacy of treaties among the cantons for the collection of import duties; it also passes upon the legitimacy of treaties among the cantons or between a canton and a foreign power. The Austrian federal system goes further in routinizing an executive procedure for receiving and passing upon every law of the member states from the standpoint of the question whether it "endangers federal interests." If challenged on this ground, an additional procedure at the state level is required.

Switzerland is a seeming exception among the well-established federal systems since its high court cannot pass on the validity of the laws of the central government, although (as the partial protector of the federal arrangent) it has the power to strike down the enactments of the member cantons. Even in that country, however, a partial substitute for judicial review of national actions is the use of the popular referendum as a method for challenging the laws that are passed by the central government.

ADMINISTRATIVE PATTERNS IN FEDERAL SYSTEMS

A main variation in the constitutional provisions for federalism is the use of the member states of a union as agents for carrying out national laws. The systems in Europe, especially Switzerland, in evolving from confederal beginnings, make extensive use of what is called "indirect federal administration." The constitutions of Austria and West Germany use that very phrase. The United States, reacting in the constitutional convention of 1787 against the Articles of Confederation, broke ground for a directly national administration of the laws of Congress to a greater extent than is usually noted, although many of the early laws provided alternatively for their enforcement through the state courts. Today important differences exist in the world among the systems that emphasize indirect or direct methods for carrying out the mandatory enactments of the central governments. Nevertheless, one of the most significant trends in the varied applications of federalism is the merging of methods.

Indirect Federal Administration in European Systems

The postwar structure of the Federal Republic of Germany illustrates the continental idea of relying widely on indirect federal administration by the merger of systems that has been mentioned. The member states in West Germany's federal scheme are charged with the duty of carrying out the federal laws as their own concern insofar as the national constitution does not otherwise determine or permit. The central government supervises the process and may send commissioners to the member states in order to ensure conformance. But the dependence upon the member states as administrative agents is qualified. Basic laws in certain fields are carried out by the central government's own administrative officers at the local as well as the higher levels. Moreover, the procedures of direct federal administration may be established by law in many fields where the national government has legislative powers. So far as the member states are asked to act as administrative agents, the indirect process is helped by the largely similar educational backgrounds of the officials at both levels. It is aided also by the fact that the constituent states are represented in the upper chamber (a preparatory rather than strictly legislative body) and share in framing the laws that often are given them to administer.

The extent of West Germany's reliance upon indirect federal administration has been shown by Roger H. Wells. A little after mid-century the Laender had 671,463 employees and the local governments 473,272. The central government (leaving out the military, postal, and railway employees) "ranks numerically well below the states and the local governments where the main burden of administration rests."[11]

11. Roger Hewes Wells, *The States in West German Federalism: A Study of Federal-State Relations 1949-1960* (New York: Bookman Associates, 1961), pp. 55, 66.

But the author notes that the agency role of the Laender is "a two-way street." Although the states are agents of the central government, "they have much influence in determining what the federal law shall be which they administer." The officials of the central government are accustomed to consult with their counterparts in the Laender when drafting laws. Moreover, "after enactment, state implementing legislation may be necessary, as well as federal administrative regulations which require Bundesrat approval."

In Switzerland the stated theory of the constitution as well as the practice is marked by a large measure of indirect federal administration. When the cantons are carrying out legislative enactments of the central government, they usually have a free hand within the basic norms. Emblematic of the spirit of the system in dealing with borderline subjects is the constitutional provision which says:

> The Confederation, within its own legislative powers, may furthermore authorize the cantons to issue regulations in fields which do not require general legislation by the Confederation itself and which actually do not fall under the jurisdiction of the cantons.

The modernized practice of indirect federal administration is also illustrated in the Austrian federal system which originally was introduced after World War I and revived after World War II. Especially interesting because in line with what is emerging in federal systems generally is the power of the central government to establish by law certain fundamental norms, leaving it to the member states to promulgate supplementary legislation and to administer the composite provisions. On a number of matters that are listed in the constitution the central government has the power to legislate but the constituent states have the power to execute. On certain matters the central government is empowered to pass laws "as to basic principles" but the states have the right to enact the "enabling legislation" and to carry out the laws. As an aspect of indirect federal administration, it should be noted that within each constituent state the head of the government and his subordinates are charged by the constitution with the duty of carrying out the central government's executive powers where national officers do not exist.

Direct Federal Administration in the United States: Wavering Changes

In the United States, despite collaborative features under the constitution, heavy stress fell upon the system of separate national and state laws and upon dual administration. The constitution was conceived and its rough-hewn purposes were shaped by men who were reacting sharply against perceived deficiencies in the Articles of Confederation. Under that earlier form of union the central government had depended upon the mediation of the state governments in vital matters such as taxation. The critics, in the words of Noah Webster in 1784, advocated a "new system which should act, not on the states, but directly on individuals, and vest in Congress all power to enforce its own laws." The new constitution was framed in the belief that indifference, incompetence, even active hostility on the part of the member states could be avoided by national arrangements that would depend as little as possible upon the state governments. This solution called not only for national powers but also for a national administration and judiciary which together would permeate the country. Such was the emphasis.

Nevertheless, from the outset, in the face of the problems of distance and poor transportation while national activities were still slight, many laws of Congress allowed citizens the option of dealing on designated matters through state officials. In those days administration was simpler; much of it indeed was performed judicially. The requirements of the time and the availability of the state courts were shown in the comment of a Pennsylvania judge in 1824: ". . . although inconvenience is no justification for usurpation of power, yet as the court does not see how this conflicts with the constitution of the United States, the inconvenience may be considered; and it would be an intolerable inconvenience, in an action for a petty penalty, to draw a man from the most remote corner of the state, to the seat of the federal judiciary."[12]

Fifteen years later, however, the already changing attitude was shown in the refusal of a state judge to handle a case that involved a lawsuit for the collection of a penalty by the national government. "The consideration of the convenience of the citizen does not weigh a feather with me," he said, adding: "I sit here to administer the laws of South Carolina; and in the discharge of my appropriate duties, find ample occupation for all my time and ample employment for all my powers. I do not come here to enforce the criminal laws of the United States, whose government in that regard is a foreign government."[13]

The shifting attitude was due in part to the mounting business in each of the two systems of courts. It was invited by the growing ease of travel. In addition, it doubtless reflected the strains that were deepening in the years before the Civil War. It was ironic though understandable that spokesmen for the area where slavery survived did on occasion extol the power and procedures of the central government under the nation's fugitive slave law. In a famous case in 1842 the real opponents were Pennsylvania and Maryland and the question was the possibility of a way "to terminate disputes and contentions which were arising and had for years arisen along the border line between them on this subject of the escape and delivering up of fugitive slaves."[14]

The double judicial system of the United States follows broadly the line between the national government's regula-

12. *Buckwalter* v. *United States,* 11 S. and R. 193 at 197 (1824).
13. *State* v. *McBride,* 1 Rice 400 at 404 (1839).
14. *Prigg* v. *Pennsylvania,* 16 Peters 539 (1842).

tory powers and the services that the central government can conduct itself or help the state and local governments in performing if they are willing to do so. Intermediate zones exist. The national courts have jurisdiction over suits between citizens in different states, administering mainly the state law that is relevant. Moreover, the state courts may have duties in handling cases that are brought to them under national laws. Thus the congressional law on the liability of interstate railroads to injured workers gave the latter the option of bringing their suits in either a national court or a state court. The Supreme Court held that the state courts must handle such suits.[15] The congressional law, it said, "is as much the policy of Connecticut as if the act had emanated from its own legislature, and should be respected accordingly in the courts of the state."

Interlevel Administrative Collaboration
in the United States

It has been noted that the United States pioneered among the world's federal systems by introducing the principle called direct federal administration. Nevertheless, as has also been noted, the state instrumentalities were used by the central government, at least as alternatives, under the laws of Congress on many matters throughout the early decades. Some of this relationship was inherent in the interlocking of levels that exist in federalism. Much of the collaboration survived, even when it was not an indispensable feature of the country's federal structure. In addition, and increasingly in recent times, the administrative machinery of the states and localities has been used under national laws. From the other side, the instrumentalities of the central government have often been enlisted by the states under their statutes.

Since administration mostly involves individuals with distinctive kinds of work to do, many of the foregoing‧ rela-

15. *Mondou* v. *New York, New Haven, and Hartford Ry.,* 223 U.S. 1 at 57 (1912).

tions involve such things as joint training (oftener the training of state and local officers under national auspices than
vice versa) and the full-time loan of individuals by one unit
of government to another, such as the instances where officers in the United States Public Health Service have served
on loan as heads of state health departments or on other
special assignments. Such interchanges have become familiar
in the United States. They promise to grow with the movement toward a fuller union among the personnel systems at
all levels. The possibilities were recognized in the launching
in 1969 of the intergovernmental affairs staff as a unit in the
Bureau of Policies and Standards of the United States Civil
Service Commission and in the passage of the Intergovernmental Personnel Act of 1970.

The patterns of collaboration from both sides are best surveyed in general terms. On the one side, the states serve administratively as agents of the central government in carrying out certain of its laws. From the other side, national officers in particular fields are empowered under state laws,
sometimes to help them incidentally in carrying out their
national duties, sometimes to make them virtually the agents
of the state in helping to achieve its purposes, but often to
mingle operations in a way that aids the central government
and the state simultaneously. Moreover, the states often act
as agents of each other under cross-investitures of power. It
is obvious that the foregoing ways of conferring authority
across the barriers of federalism (between the nation and a
state or among states) are of many kinds with varying de-
grees of responsibility and power.

Sometimes the cross-jurisdictional conferral of power ap-
plies to all persons who occupy a certain kind of position,
whether under the nation or under a state government.
Sometimes a particular person is invested with the authority;
thus he may be named as a collaborator, or may be licensed
or deputized or empowered under some other title. These
formal cross-jurisdictional conferrals of authority merge into

a variety of working relations between the central government and the states where their personnel are mingled. Often such personnel merely join in an investigation. This situation is at the other extreme from the sorts of relations that are involved where the nation or a state, as the case may be, accepts as binding an inspection or certification that is made by the other.

CONCLUSION

The United States pioneered for the world in using, indeed almost inventing, direct federal administration. Nevertheless, throughout its history under the constitution the nation has used the administrative facilities of the state governments for many purposes; the states under their laws have drawn support from national auspices. The gains often are so mutual that it is almost impossible to say which level is helped the more. These collaborative practices have been in common with the spirit of indirect federal administration, along the lines noted in the European systems. Even more importantly, as will be seen, the growing use of national grants-in-aid for permissive services is moving toward the strengthening of indirect federal administration in the United States.

But the regulatory side of government, where laws are mandatory and coercive, involves a separation of the jurisdictions of the central government and the states. The scope of the nation's control is becoming more complete in certain fields, in part through a broader use of the power to regulate interstate commerce. In these circumstances, while it is possible for state control to be authorized, the overarching power is national.

II

Federal Relations in Administering Regulatory Powers

THE GOVERNMENT'S REGULATORY WORK must be distinguished from the permissive services that abound in modern states. Regulation is mandatory, with penalties. Often, it is true, the control is promotive rather than restrictive in its purposes and in its effects. Many types of service, on the other hand, act as guides, although legally they need not be followed. Basically, however, regulatory functions differ from the service activities where the penalties for violations are only incidental so far as they exist at all. This chapter deals with the coercively regulatory activities of the central government in federal systems. But as will be noted, the achievement of fully comprehensive regulation of many important matters often leaves open the way for state governments that care to act within this framework.

The importance of mandatory controls is not belittled by the fact that persuasion through financial support and other inducements is part of the apparatus of progress in flexible societies. In future decades, facing among other problems an endangered environment that calls for comprehensive regulation as well as costly public works, the scope of the central government's punitive commands must grow.

In the United States the constitution gives Congress a

sweeping—indeed almost an unlimited—power to tax and to borrow. Along with this it confers the power to "provide for the common defence and general welfare of the United States." The spending power of Congress rests on the latter phrase. Far-reaching, too, is the range of purposes that Congress may support under the so-called property power that the constitution defines as the congressional power "to dispose of and make all needful rules and regulations respecting the territory or other property belonging to the United States." But none of these powers—to tax, to spend, and to dispose of property—extends to coercively regulatory activities by the national government. Later chapters will deal with the property power and the spending power as main pillars in the structure of intergovernmental relations in the United States.

CONSTITUTIONAL BASES OF NATIONAL REGULATORY POWERS

Federal constitutions generally give more regulatory powers to the central government than does that of the United States. Here, as Woodrow Wilson truly said, the charter approved in 1789 was wrung by grinding necessity from a reluctant people. Its main draftsmen were national in their outlook for it was a nation they were building. As realists, however, they confined their draft to the things that were indispensable but in language that mostly proved capable of growth through interpretation and usage.

Later federal constitutions empowered the central governments more fully and explicitly. Canada, for example, entrusts the Dominion's parliament with such wide fields as the regulation of trade and commerce, navigation and shipping, and banking, in addition to the criminal law and marriage and divorce. In Australia, although the range given to the central government is relatively narrow in accord with a traditional view of federalism, the national powers include jurisdiction over "marriage . . . divorce and matrimonial causes; and, in relation thereto, parental rights, and the custody and guardianship of infants." It is unnecessary to speak of the European federal systems or of a modern scheme like that of India; the norm-setting power of their central governments has already been noted as a feature of their constitutions. Moreover, it is beside the point to add details about the way in which the Latin American federations give the national government jurisdiction as broad as the civil law and the law of trade and commerce.

National Regulatory Powers Other Than the Regulation of Commerce

In the United States the crucial role of the commerce power as the basis for much of the nation's regulatory action does not denigrate the importance of certain other controls that are expressly given by the constitution. They deal with the monetary system, the postal service, weights and measures, patents and copyrights, the naturalization of aliens, a uniform rule for bankruptcy, the admission of new states, certain phases of the conduct of national elections, the government of a district for the national capital, the steps that may be necessary to ensure that "full faith and credit shall be given in each state to the public acts, records, and judicial proceedings of every other state," and the possible need for congressional legislation in giving effect to the fundamental guarantees of the Fourteenth Amendment. "No state," it says, "shall make or enforce any law which shall abridge the privileges or immunities of citizens of the United States; nor shall any State deprive any person of life, liberty, or property, without due process of law; nor deny to any person within its jurisdiction the equal protection of the laws." This lengthy amendment (only the salient clauses of which have been quoted) concludes by saying that "The Congress shall have power to enforce, by appropriate legislation, the provisions of this article."

The expressly granted authority of the central government touches matters of the highest importance. The war power includes the power to declare war, to raise and support armed forces, to provide for the organization and discipline of the militia in the states, and the central government's right to call on the latter for help in executing the national laws, suppressing insurrection, or repelling invasions. The power to make treaties, exercised by the President with the consent of the Senate, is already broad and likely to widen further with international practice. In 1920, for example, the Supreme Court upheld a congressional law that was based upon a treaty with Canada for the mutual safeguarding of migratory birds.[1] In this situation the resort of Congress to the treaty power was a second and successful attempt to find a basis for legislation; previously it had been checked by the courts in its attempted use of the commerce power as it was then interpreted.[2] Here is a national interest, said the court in the later case, that "can be protected only by national action in concert with that of another power."

The subsequent decisions of the Supreme Court have dealt with "executive agreements" rather than treaties as such. In upholding such agreements the court has spoken of "the very delicate, plenary and exclusive power of the President."[3] The court in this opinion came close to putting foreign affairs in a unique position constitutionally, saying: "The broad statement that the federal government can exercise no powers except those specifically enumerated in the Constitution, and such implied powers as are necessary and proper to carry into effect the enumerated powers, is categorically true only in respect of our internal affairs."

Generally speaking, the mere fact that a power is given to the national government does not make it exclusively na-

1. *Missouri* v. *Holland,* 252 U.S. 416 at 435 (1920).
2. *United States* v. *Shauver,* 214 Fed. Rep. 154 (1914).
3. *United States* v. *Curtiss-Wright Export Corporation,* 299 U.S. 304 at 320 (1936).

tional. The fact that the national government has exercised a power does not abolish existing nor preclude new state legislation so long as there is no inconsistency with the actions of the national government. This feature in the constitutional system of the United States has invited the existence of parallel bodies of law which in turn have often emphasized the need for administrative cooperation. The main concern of this chapter, however, is the extent of the congressional power to pass mandatory laws.

From the outset the central government's control over maritime matters and admiralty was substantially complete. The sound justification was the critical need for uniformity in matters where diversity would be especially vexatious. "The definite object of the grant," said the Supreme Court, "was to commit direct control to the Federal Government; to relieve maritime commerce from the unnecessary burdens and disadvantages incident to discordant legislation; and to establish, so far as practicable, harmonious and uniform rules applicable throughout every part of the Union."[4] In this spirit the handling of the claims of injured harbor workers was treated as exclusively national.[5]

When a national banking system was created early in the country's history the Supreme Court found no express basis for it.[6] Instead, it fell back on the implications of the constitution, fortified by the so-called elastic clause, which says that Congress can pass "all laws which shall be necessary and proper for carrying into execution the foregoing powers, and all other powers vested by this constitution" in the national government. The words should be construed, said Chief Justice John Marshall for the court, in light of the fact that "a thing may be necessary, very necessary, absolutely or indispensably necessary." The ruling upheld the bank's legitimacy. It is relevant to add that when the national banking

---

4. *Knickerbocker Ice Company* v. *Stewart,* 253 U.S. 149 at 164 (1920).
5. *Southern Pacific Co.* v. *Jensen,* 244 U.S. 205 (1917).
6. *McCulloch* v. *Maryland,* 4 Wheaton 315 at 413 (1819).

system was re-created the state banks were not ousted. Instead, Congress used its taxing power to prevent them from issuing notes that were a form of money.[7]

The Supreme Court said: "Congress may restrain, by suitable enactments, the circulation as money of any notes not issued under its own authority." The court added: "Without this poser, indeed, its attempt to secure a sound and uniform currency of the country must be futile." It upheld the intentionally prohibitory tax upon state bank notes. The state banking systems survived, however, despite the creation of the Federal Reserve System and its growing role as a main regulator of the country's economy. This system is open to the state banks, but not all of them have chosen to join it.

The growing array of activities that have to do with credit have not been made exclusively national. An example of dual control under a congressional law is the Consumer Credit Protection Act of 1968.[8] Creditors are still subject to state laws, if consistent, and the statute exempts transactions if "under the law of that state that class of transactions is subject to requirements substantially similar" to those that are imposed under the national law and "there is adequate provision for enforcement."

The Attempt to Create a National
"Common Law" for Business

Before speaking about national regulation in the United States under the commerce power of Congress a word should be said about the existence throughout the English-speaking world of the body of legal rules called the common law. It had evolved slowly in England through many centuries. Largely it was the handiwork of courts through an accretion of precedents. It was enriched by principles that were drawn from the customary dealings of merchants. It was supplemented, too, by the body of rules called equity that sought to prevent in-

7. *Veazie Bank* v. *Fenno*, 8 Wallace 533 at 549 (1869).
8. Public Law 90-321, 82 Stat. 146, May 29, 1968.

juries of a kind for which money damages would not be a recompense after the harm had been done. In the North American colonies the common law was dominant. It helped to provide a doctrinal unity in the period before independence, and its standardizing influence survived in the states. For a long time it was the major element of civil law.

With the passing of time new problems brought a growing volume of statute law. The national courts faced increasingly divergent doctrines in handling law suits between citizens of different states. This jurisdiction, embodied in the constitution, was partly intended to ensure impartiality. The law to be applied was that of one or another state, whichever was more relevant. Meanwhile, the state judiciaries were growing apart; the laws of the states were diverging. In 1842 the Supreme Court took an attempted step toward uniformity by announcing that the national judiciary would develop its own body of law in deciding certain types of disputes between litigants resident in different states.[9] At the time interest in the problem of legal uniformity was growing throughout the western world. Justice Story and his colleagues on the Supreme Court in 1842 hoped that the state judiciaries would follow the doctrines that were developed nationally in handling disputes between citizens of different states.

This hope was not realized, and in 1938 the Supreme Court renounced the attempt.[10] It said that the law to be applied in controversies between citizens of different states was that of one or the other of the states of residence, whichever was appropriate. Thus ended an experiment that had been announced almost a century earlier as a movement toward uniformity. The effort, in effect, had merely provided an additional body of doctrine without lessening the variations among the state judiciaries, now well established and proud in their separate jurisdictions. The Supreme Court confessed

9. *Swift* v. *Tyson,* 16 Peters 1 (1842).
10. *Erie Railroad Co.* v. *Tompkins,* 304 U.S. 64 at 71 (1938).

its own error; it said: "If only a question of statutory construction were involved, we should not be prepared to abandon a doctrine so widely applied throughout nearly a century. But the unconstitutionality of the course pursued has now been made clear and compels us to do so."

The frustration of the hopes of Justice Story and his associates was due in part to the growing strength and self-reliance of the high courts in many states. More fundamentally, perhaps, it was due to the growth of state legislation. The slowly evolving precedents of the common law were being supplanted by statute laws, often novel, as public policy pushed forward unevenly in different states. Moreover, the divergence was increased often by the movement for codification. These formulations differed from state to state much more than had the judicial applications of the common law. After 1890 an organized movement began for the drafting of uniform laws on certain matters for voluntary adoption by the states. A later chapter will appraise this effort. It will comment also on the important role of administrators at different levels in promoting the use of common standards. Many of the norms are woven into the fabric of the statute laws of the states. But a basic approach had to be through the power of Congress to regulate interstate and foreign commerce.

THE COMMERCE CLAUSE: A MAIN BASIS
FOR NATIONAL CONTROLS

In domestic controls generally the national power to regulate interstate commerce is the main basis for mandatory action. This power touches nearly every aspect of life. But "interstate" may be construed as a limiting word. Mostly the nation's power in the field of commerce is concurrent with that of the state governments unless Congress shows expressly that it is assuming exclusive power over a phase of interstate commerce. Sometimes it seeks to extend its regulatory control into the field of intrastate commerce. A major question, as will be seen, is the extent to which this field can be regulated nationally because of its connection with interstate commerce. On this point, increasingly, turn some of the most significant issues of national control.

The congressional power to regulate commerce among the states has two main aspects. One purpose is to ensure the existence of a nationwide market with freedom of trade among the parts of the country. That side of the power is negative; it is a restriction on state action. The other side is positive. From the outset in 1789, it has provided a main basis for national control of economic matters. As a legal foundation for mandatory regulation the congressional power over interstate commerce is not less momentous because it remained largely unused for nearly a century.

The Negative Side: The Commerce Clause as a Restriction

For a long time it was the negative side of the commerce clause, protecting a growing economy against state barriers, that gave main importance to the commerce power domestically. In 1824 a notable decision of the Supreme Court invalidated a law of New York State that had given Robert Fulton and his associates a monopoly (for a period of years not yet ended) in operating steamboats on the waters of the state. This law was viewed as a contract. The state was beginning to regret the agreement into which it had entered. It was helpless, however, in the face of the provision in the national constitution that no state can pass a "law impairing the obligation of contracts." The national government is not bound by a like restriction. The Supreme Court, on the basis of the negative side of the commerce power, was able to outlaw the steamboat monopoly.[11] The implications were far-reaching. They assured a wide area of freedom from state interference with the movement of things and persons.

11. *Gibbons* v. *Ogden,* 9 Wheaton 1 (1824).

Almost at the same time as the above decision, another landmark case helped to establish the principle that the national government's commerce power, on its negative side, forbids an improper degree of state interference with movements from state to state. This second ruling invalidated a state's attempt to levy import duties on goods brought into the state.[12] The basic ground of the decision was the idea of protecting the national marketplace against state barriers. The court's application of this principle was made easier by the express constitutional proviso that "no state shall, without the consent of the Congress, lay any imposts or duties on imports or exports, except what may be absolutely necessary for executing its inspection law." The basic objective of liberating the national market from state interference was put in its historical setting by the court's comment (speaking through Chief Justice John Marshall) that "from the vast inequality between the different states of the confederacy, as to commercial advantages, few subjects were viewed with deeper interest, or excited more irritation, than the manner in which the several States exercised, or seemed disposed to exercise, the power of laying duties on imports."

The ban on state interference with interstate commerce has never been absolute. In the early decades under the national constitution, as has been noted, a heavy stress did fall on the need to establish the principle of liberating interstate trade from state restrictions. That doctrine eased a bit before the middle of the nineteenth century. Even while John Marshall was chief justice the judicial rulings swung somewhat in favor of upholding state and local action, in line with a concurrent view of regulatory powers. State controls were upheld in the so-called License Tax cases.[13] Even earlier the Supreme Court had declined to invalidate Philadelphia's scheme of port regulation that included the licensing of pilots. A majority of the court concurred in the ruling that

12. *Brown* v. *Maryland,* 12 Wheaton 419 at 438 (1827).
13. *License Tax Cases,* 72 U.S. 462 (1867).

"the mere grant to Congress of the power to regulate commerce, did not deprive the States of power to regulate pilots." The majority believed that, although Congress had legislated on the subject, it had done so in terms that showed the wish "to leave its regulation to the several states."[14]

Later, although retaining the judicial power to pass on the property of state taxation and other actions that infringe unduly upon interstate commerce, the national courts took account of the frequent need to strike a balance between the financial needs of the state governments as against the ideal of a national marketplace. This outlook did not reach its peak until well after the Civil War. Even late in the eighteen-seventies, when some of the state governments were becoming increasingly active in behalf of farmers as a disadvantaged group, the Supreme Court upheld the Illinois law that regulated the grain elevators as to their charges and other matters.[15] This stand was taken, however, before the heyday of the belief, dominant for a time in the country's thinking, that things mostly should be left for adjustment through competitive forces. That view did not give way until the third decade of this century.

The Positive Side of the Commerce Clause: Its Expanding Role

National regulation of economic matters, in contrast with the negative role of the commerce clause in preventing governmental action, appeared late in the nineteenth century. A start was made in 1884 by the animal industry act for the control of diseases among cattle. The law's punitive restrictions applied mainly to international trade, but the interstate shipment of diseased cattle was forbidden. A collaborative program with states developed; it depended partially upon their coercive powers. The compulsory dipping of cattle became widespread. The national government under agree-

14. *Cooley* v. *Board of Wardens*, 12 Howard 298 at 320 (1851).
15. *Munn* v. *Illinois*, 94 U.S. 113 (1877).

ments with individual states undertook through them to compensate the owners of diseased animals that were killed as a corrective measure. Step by step, county by county through many decades, the disease-free area was extended. National and state personnel, though legally separate, usually mingled in the operations. At the start of the new bureau of animal industry in 1884 there were at most a score of national inspectors with a hundred thousand dollars at their disposal "to prevent the exportation of diseased cattle, and to provide means for the extirpation of pleuro-pneumonia and other contagious diseases among domestic animals."[16] These developments were emblematic of the national government's cautious entrance into the field of positive controls.

Meanwhile, widespread state action on railroading preceded the incipient regulation by Congress of its interstate aspects. The decisive push toward regulation by the central government came in 1886. The Supreme Court's contribution was negatively instrumental.[17] It struck down the attempt of Illinois to deal with the problem. The court said "it is not, and never has been, the deliberate opinion of a majority of this court that a statute of a state which attempts to regulate the fares and charges by railroad companies within its limits, for a transportation which constitutes a part of commerce among the states, is a valid law." The passage by Congress of the Interstate Commerce Act in the next year would doubtless have come at some time. The court's decision in 1886 made inevitable its almost immediate enactment.

During the foregoing decades, especially in the seventies and eighties, agricultural discontent had been rising. The restiveness that was shown in the farming areas was provoked in part by complaints about unduly high railroad rates. It

16. 48th Congress, Vol. 23, ch. 60, May 29, 1884.
17. *Wabash, St. Louis, and Pacific Railway Co.* v. *Illinois*, 118 U.S. 557 at 575 (1886).

came also in part from the practice of rebates to particular shippers. Partly it reflected the belief that certain areas in the country were neglected. Congress began to inquire into these complaints. It was at that stage that a Senate committee even broached the idea of nationalizing the country's railroads.

The tide was swelling toward the national government, changing many boundary marks in the country's federalism. Soon to be enacted was the antitrust law of 1890, although, narrowly applied at first, its enforcement was destined to lag for many years. The Supreme Court slowed things in 1895 by drawing the distinction between manufacturing and commerce, saying that otherwise "comparatively little of business operations and affairs would be left for state control."[18] The vitality of railroad control through the Interstate Commerce Commission also waited for later amendments, especially a supplementary law in 1908.

The necessary force for congressional action had gathered momentum cumulatively. State control of foods had begun to appear in the eighties: in 1881 in New York, New Jersey, and Michigan, and in the next year in Massachusetts. These and other states became warm advocates of national legislation as the way to overcome the frustration of state efforts. By 1903 the state departments generally were throwing their weight behind the passage of a national law. It was needed, said the National Association of State Dairy and Food Departments, "to harmonize the discordant provisions of our state laws, and, like a cap-sheaf, perfect American food legislation."

Further decisions helped to open the way in other domains. In motor transport, the 1925 decision of the Supreme Court that invalidated a state law because it impinged unduly upon interstate commerce presaged the later passage of a national law for the interstate regulation of common carriers by road.[19] The holding by the Supreme Court that a state could not regulate the interstate transmission of elec-

18. *United States* v. *E. C. Knight Co.,* 156 U.S. 1 at 16 (1895).
19. *Buck* v. *Kuykendall,* 267 U.S. 307 (1925).

tricity in wholesale quantities made inevitable the national control in that field that soon followed.[20] A somewhat similar sequence came in handling the interstate movements of natural gas.[21]

The progress of national regulation, even of interstate commerce, was still checked by the idea that on the positive side the purpose of the regulation is to "cleanse" commerce. Some people even went to the length of arguing that Congress did not have the right to prohibit movements in interstate commerce. The eclipse of this idea, however, was shown in 1903 when a majority of the Supreme Court (with four members dissenting) upheld a congressional law that barred lottery tickets from interstate and foreign commerce as well as from the mails.[22] The majority opinion declared that the power to regulate commerce among the states is "plenary." A few years later, with echoes of the view that it is enough to consider the constitutionality of legislation "when we must do so," the court upheld the early legislation for the protection of consumers against adulterated or diseased or otherwise harmful foods and drugs. The rationale was the protection of the recipient, sustained by the argument that the harm was increased by the interstate movement of the harmful substance.[23]

THE TEMPORARY JUDICIAL CHALLENGE OF
NATIONAL ECONOMIC CONTROLS

A decision that delayed national action for many years was the Supreme Court's invalidation in 1918 of the law against child labor that Congress had passed two years before.[24] It sought to bar from interstate commerce things produced by

20. *Public Utilities Commission* v. *Attleboro Steam and Electric Company*, 273 U.S. 83 (1927).
21. *State Corporation Commission* v. *Wichita Gas Co.*, 290 U.S. 561 (1934).
22. *Champion* v. *Ames*, 188 U.S. 321 (1903).
23. *Hipolite Egg Co.* v. *United States*, 220 U.S. 45 (1911).
24. *Hammer* v. *Dagenhart*, 247 U.S. 251 at 276 (1918).

children under the age of fourteen in manufacturing and under sixteen in mining and when all under sixteen worked more than six days a week and between seven o'clock at night and six in the morning. The court's adverse decision was made by a vote of five to four. The prompt attempt of Congress to outlaw child labor through the use of the taxing power was declared invalid by the Supreme Court four years later.[25] A subsequent effort to amend the constitution failed to get the requisite number of state ratifications. The country's mood was stiffening in the twenties, and national control of child labor did not come until the following decade.

Meanwhile, during the early stage of a momentous advance in public policy, a majority of the Supreme Court contended for a time against the trend that was called the New Deal. It struck down several congressional enactments. The most notable of these was the law of 1933 known as the national recovery act. More than six hundred codes, drafted cooperatively in the country's industries and intended to promote the conditions of fair competition, had gone into effect when the suit that became the test case reached the Supreme Court in 1935. Ironically, it arose in a minor industry—the selling of live poultry.

It was not wholly unfair that a petty industry—the selling of live poultry—became the test case. Code-making as a strategy for combating the economic depression had indeed gone out of bounds. It had spread far beyond the basic industries where it was truly appropriate. It is fair to add that a tightening of the process had already begun at the time when the Supreme Court struck down the system as a whole.

The Supreme Court unanimously invalidated the law as a whole.[26] It was lacking in standards, said the court. "In determining how far the federal government may go in controlling intrastate transactions upon the ground that they 'affect' interstate commerce" the court added, "there is a necessary

25. *Bailey* v. *Drexel Furniture Company*, 259 U.S. 20 (1922).
26. *Schechter Poultry Corporation* v. *U.S.*, 295 U.S. 495 (1935).

and well-established distinction between direct and indirect effects." This adverse ruling (soon to be modified) did not deny that the nation's commerce power can properly take account of the direct effects of intrastate commerce on that which is interstate.

The turning point had not yet come. Almost simultaneously a majority in the Supreme Court invalidated a congressional law for the retirement of railroad workers. The decision held that the law was "in no proper sense a regulation of the activity of interstate transportation."[27] In the following year the majority in the court ruled against the constitutionality of the labor provisions of a congressional law for the stabilization of bituminous coal mining.[28] The opinion declared that "the employment of men, the fixing of their wages, hours of labor and working conditions, the bargaining in respect of these things—whether carried on separately or collectively—each and all constitute intercourse for the purposes of production, not of trade. . . ." Such aspects of production, it said, lay beyond the reach of the congressional power to regulate interstate commerce.

THE RELEASE OF THE COMMERCE POWER

The turn came in the late thirties. On the surface it was made possible by a shift of viewpoint on the part of one member of the Supreme Court. At bottom it represented a major and probably lasting change in the interpretation of the constitution. This fact was evident in the five decisions in 1937 that upheld the National Labor Relations Act, passed by Congress two years before. These companion cases involved a varied array of concerns: one of the country's largest steel companies; a manufacturer of clothing whose

27. *Railroad Retirement Board* v. *Alton Railroad Co.*, 295 U.S. 330 at 374 (1935).
28. *Carter* v. *Carter Coal Company*, 298 U.S. 238 at 303 (1936).

products were sold widely; a large concern that manufactured trailers; a motor bus company; and the Associated Press.

The argument for the validity of the national law, and for the Labor Board machinery that it created, rested in part on the fact that labor disputes are an inhibiting burden on interstate commerce and that this burden may be lessened by the methods of adjustment that are created by the law. The court said in the main case: "Although activities may be intrastate in character when separately considered, if they have such a close and substantial relation to interstate commerce that their control is essential or appropriate to protect that commerce from burdens and obstructions, Congress cannot be denied the power to exercise that control."[29]

A qualification was added that made the Supreme Court's support of the law a bit less than sweeping. "Undoubtedly," said the court, "the scope of this power must be considered in the light of our dual system of government and may not be extended so as to embrace effects upon interstate commerce so indirect and remote that to embrace them, in view of our complex society, would effectively obliterate the distinction between what is national and what is local and create a completely centralized government." It left a task for Congress and for the courts in the years ahead by adding: "the question is necessarily one of degree."

When the bituminous coal measure was re-enacted without the labor provisions but still with the purpose of stabilizing a distressed industry, the Supreme Court upheld the abridged version in 1940 with a single dissent. "To invalidate this act," said the court, "we would have to deny the existence of power on the part of Congress under the commerce clause to deal directly and specifically with those forces which in its judgment should not be permitted to dislocate an important segment of our economy and to disrupt

29. *National Labor Relations Board* v. *Jones & Laughlin Steel Corporation,* 301 U.S. 1 at 37 (1937).

and burden interstate channels of trade.''[30] The revised law that was upheld in these terms had not reached the Supreme Court until after the major shift (already noted) had taken place in the outlook of its majority members on the question of constitutionality.

Further confirmation of the shift was at hand. More sweeping was the Supreme Court's language in 1941 when it upheld the Fair Labor Standards Act that Congress had passed a few years before. The issue before the court involved a double question: "whether Congress has constitutional power to prohibit the shipment in interstate commerce of lumber manufactured by employees whose wages are less than a prescribed minimum or whose weekly hours of labor at that wage are less than a prescribed minimum, and, second, whether it has power to prohibit the employment of workmen in the production of goods 'for interstate commerce' at other than prescribed wages and hours.''[31] In answering both questions affirmatively, the decision said that "The motive and purpose of a regulation of interstate commerce are matters for the legislative judgment upon the exercise of which the Constitution places no restriction and over which the courts are given no control."

The surviving question is whether the state control will be sufficiently watchful. In 1960 a majority of the Supreme Court held that the action of Congress in 1945 did not deprive the people in the states generally of the protection of the Federal Trade Commission. Moreover, although the earlier case had reinstated the state agencies as the principal regulatory control for the insurance industry, it was emblematic that Congress in the sixties directed the Transportation Department to study the system for motor vehicle compensation throughout the country.

It is unnecessary to mention other decisions that have upheld the widened discretion of Congress under the commerce

30. *Sunshine Anthracite Coal Company* v. *Adkins,* 310 U.S. 381 at 395 (1940).
31. *United States* v. *Darby,* 312 U.S. 100 at 113 and 115 (1941).

power. Much still depends upon the skillful phrasing by which the regulatory laws of Congress deal with the interactions between interstate and intrastate commerce. The language of recent statutes varies in its range. The source of coercive power in most situations is still the mandated right of Congress to regulate commerce with foreign nations and among the states. Only lately has the regulation of interstate commerce been broadened by law in ways that allow the national control of commerce to regulate the whole of certain fields of activity. Even then, as will be noted, scope is left usually for states that care to act.

A FULLER COVERAGE FOR NATIONAL CONTROLS

Most of the important regulatory laws that are passed by Congress under the commerce power have deliberately stopped short of occupying the whole field that they enter. Moreover, they vary in the effectiveness with which they provide for administrative collaboration with the states; some indeed are silent on the question. But voluntary cooperation between separate jurisdictions is not the answer in the crucial regulatory fields. In the future it will not offend the essence of federalism in the United States to make many if not all of the national controls comprehensive in their coverage and universally binding.

Problems of Coverage in Labor Legislation

It is for Congress in the first instance to say whether a law passed under the power to regulate interstate commerce is inclusive even within the scope of that power. Ticklish issues arose under the National Labor Relations Act. In 1963 the Supreme Court said: "This Court has consistently declared that in passing the National Labor Relations Act, Congress intended to and did vest in the Board the fullest jurisdictional breadth constitutionally permissible under the Commerce clause."[32] It quoted from a previous decision that said: "Congress has explicitly regulated not merely transactions or goods in interstate commerce but activities which in isolation might be deemed to be merely local but in the interlacings of business across state lines adversely affect such commerce." The national board chose not to exercise the full extent of its possible jurisdiction. Instead, its rules took account of the scale and nature of the business operations within which each labor dispute arose. The board declined to handle controversies in concerns below a certain size; it avoided certain minor types of activity altogether.

This self-denying policy of the national board is defensible only if comparable state agencies are adequately empowered and if the working relations between the national and state bodies are defined by agreements that clarify the law and facilitate the assignment and handling of individual cases. Otherwise, a "no-man's land" exists where employees and employers (even in interstate commerce) are denied access to the national tribunal and yet are unable to turn to the states for alternative relief. Fortunately this no-man's land was finally eliminated by an amendment to the original act. It empowered the state to exercise jurisdiction in situations where the national board declines to act for reasons of size or otherwise. The amendment was a step in the right direction. Nevertheless, it did not provide the complete coverage that is needed in labor disputes.

Full National Control but with
Leeway for State Action

The question, as has been said, is the completeness of the coverage when mandatory controls are needed. Many growing problems in federal systems like that of the United States call increasingly for a type of regulatory action that is more than permissive or partial. It will often leave room for

32. *National Labor Relations Board* v. *Reliance Fuel Co.,* 371 U.S. 224 at 226 (1963).

the substitution of state control, but in any case the requirements must be exacting and comprehensive.

Applied science already has made some activities so universal, so disregardful of state boundaries, that the essential
controls at least must be comprehensive; they cannot be confined to interstate commerce even when this basis for action
is taken broadly. Such is the domain of radio and television.
The courts have held that the crucial regulation must be national and inclusive.[33] Realistically, the same can be said for
aeronautics. In this field, however, many of the states did
pass regulatory laws and set up their own administrative
agencies for intrastate air commerce. Later they revised their
requirements in ways that adopted the national standards
and administration for such things as the licensing of planes
and pilots. Some scope remained for state policies, such as
prohibitions against racial discrimination in the hiring of
crews.[34] The court upheld the latter on the ground that "not
only is the hiring within a State of an employee, even for an
interstate job, a much more localized matter than the transportation of passengers from State to State, but more significantly the threat of diverse and conflicting regulation of hiring practices is virtually nonexistent."

Even in something as pervasive as atomic energy there is
scope for collateral state action. A 1959 amendment to the
basic congressional law of 1946 (often called the "Federal-
State Amendment") added an elaborate section to the law.
It authorized the Atomic Energy Commission to enter into
agreements with the governor of any state for the discon-
tinuance of the commission's regulatory authority over certain matters. It said that "during the duration of such an
agreement it is recognized that the State shall have authority
to regulate the materials covered by the agreement for the
protection of the public health and safety from radiation

33. *Dumont Laboratories, Inc.* v. *Carroll,* 86 F 2nd 813 (1950).
34. *Colorado Anti-Discrimination Commission et al.* v. *Continental Air Lines,*
372 U.S. 714 at 721 (1963).

hazards."[35] The law also authorized the performing of inspections or other functions on a "cooperative" basis. It opened the way for the training of state and local personnel with attention to the added expenses for the state that might result from the collaboration. Soon after the enactment of the 1959 amendment an advisory committee of state officials met with the commission to talk about its proposed criteria. In their final form the criteria declared that any "state regulatory program shall be designed to protect the health and safety of the people against radiation hazards, thereby encouraging the constructive uses of radiation."

An illustration of the developing relationships was an agreement entered into by New Hampshire in 1966 under which the national body transferred to that state's division of public health services "certain licensing and control authority concerned with by-product, source, and special nuclear materials in quantities not sufficient to form a critical mass." The state legislature had already authorized the making of the agreement. As these arrangements spread among a majority of the states it was customary for the Atomic Energy Commission to confer with the signatory states at least twice a year. In addition it was authorized by the law itself to provide training for any state employees who were involved, with the possibility of helping to meet the additional costs that a state might incur.

As for the working of the system of agreements under the national law of 1959, the chairman of New York State's atomic and space development authority said: "Far from becoming a tool of the federal government, our experience has been that, by entering into our agreement, we have increased our stature and our influence in national nuclear regulatory affairs."

In certain types of comprehensive national action the commerce power of Congress provides the legal basis. An example is the scheme of so-called agricultural adjustment with

35. Public Law 86-373, 73 Stat. 688 at 689, September 23, 1959.

acreage limits for certain crops imposed with compensatory benefits as a way of bettering the position of farming. A basic law was passed in 1938 after the Supreme Court had invalidated the original statute. The 1938 law was upheld by the Supreme Court in terms that went beyond the question of interstate commerce. It approved a penalty that was imposed upon a farmer for planting in excess of his acreage quota, even though the produce was consumed by his cattle on the farm itself.[36] The court noted that "the wheat industry has been a problem industry for some years," adding: "One of the primary purposes of the act in question was to increase the market price of wheat, and to that end to limit the volume thereof that could affect the market." Almost at the same time the Supreme Court upheld the nearly comprehensive scope of the marketing agreements act that Congress had passed late in the thirties. "The commerce power," said the court, "is not confined in its exercise to the regulation of commerce among the states . . . the reach of that power extends to those intrastate activities which in a substantial way interfere with or obstruct the exercise of the granted power. . . ."[37]

The congressional law of 1967 called the Wholesome Meat Act signalized a new kind of inclusiveness for national controls.[38] The beginnings of mandatory regulation with regular inspections at the main packing establishments had been introduced in 1906 by a statute under the interstate commerce power.[39] Unfortunately, consumers were thrown off guard by the passage of this act and the national pure food and drug act that won its way to the statute books at almost the same time. Many people, perhaps most people, assumed that they were protected by a universal system. Yet even decades later as much as half of the country's meat supply

---

36. *Wickard* v. *Filburn,* 317 U.S. 111 at 125 and 128 (1942).
37. *United States* v. *Wrightwood Dairy Company,* 315 U.S. 110 at 119 (1942).
38. Public Law 90-201, 81 Stat. 584, December 15, 1967.
39. *Journal of Public Law,* XIII, No. 1 (1964), 189-221.

was produced and sold within individual states and was not subject to national inspection. The revelations in the sixties that led to the new law showed that there were nearly fifteen thousand plants which were processing meat for intrastate sale. Even at that late date these places were the source of 15 per cent of the slaughtered meat and 25 per cent of the processed meat. In many states no inspection existed; in none was it up to the national standards.

The 1967 statute was the answer. In its first year more than seven hundred meat packing and processing plants ceased to operate. The new law said that the central government would take over all meat inspection in any state that within three years had not adopted standards at least equal to those established under the national law. Meanwhile, twenty-eight states had entered into agreements with the national government to upgrade their meat inspection standards. It is noteworthy that in this whole affair, which involves a national law with a potentially complete coverage, the states are helped by grants-in-aid from the central government in bringing their standards for control up to the national level.

The significance of the 1967 law on meat packing is its comprehensiveness, yet the law leaves room for state control. It says that the national government shall "cooperate with the appropriate State agency in developing and administering a State meat inspection program in any State which has enacted a State meat inspection law that imposes mandatory ante mortem and post mortem inspection, reinspection, and sanitation requirements that are at least equal to those" under the national law. But the statute also says that (after notice to the state governor and consultation with an advisory committee) the national government shall take charge in any state which "does not take action to prevent such endangering of the public health within a reasonable time" after receiving the notice. The foregoing statutory provisions were elaborated in administrative regulations that were issued after a provisional notice and an extensive consultative process.[40] Most of the states were slow to comply even after additional leeway had been given. Some critics said that the availability of national inspection for the intrastate phase was an inducement for state inaction. Fundamentally, however, the situation seemed ripe for a comprehensively national system of inspection.

Poultry inspection on a continuous basis under the national power over interstate commerce goes back to 1957. This field had already become a mass industry, in part through the use of medicated feeds that prevented the outbreak of disease in large flocks. High-speed processing was helped by mechanical inventions. New sanitary problems, however, followed the technological inventions. A corrective was sought in the Wholesome Poultry Products Act of 1968 (amending a measure for poultry inspection), which declared that the regulated things are either in interstate commerce or substantially affect such commerce so that the central government may take appropriate action "to prevent and eliminate burdens upon such commerce, to effectively regulate such commerce, and to protect the health and welfare of consumers."[41] The law authorized the national government to act if a state failed to develop or was not enforcing requirements at least equal to the standards of the national law. Especially significant in the present context is the provision that, in the absence of adequate state controls for intrastate operations, the nation's regulatory supervision extends to operations even when wholly within a single state. It should be added that the 1968 law on wholesome poultry provided for cooperation with the states, saying that in carrying out the act the national authorities may "conduct such examinations, investigations, and inspections . . . through any officer or employee of any state or territory" who is "commissioned" nationally for the purpose.

40. *Federal Register,* XXXV, No. 193 (October 3, 1970), 15552–617.
41. Public Law 90-492, 82 Stat. 791, August 18, 1968.

The problems at hand are illustrated in regulating safety and health conditions in coal mines. The rigorous congressional law that won its way to the statute books in 1969 after a bitter controversy with mine-owners was prompted in part by the record of many deplorable accidents. The new law, among many far-reaching requirements, said that each mine should be inspected four times a year from the safety standpoint, with a more frequent visitation of mines with a poor record; but the Secretary of the Interior was quoted at the time of the law's enactment as saying: "We can't possibly hope to be adequately staffed for full enforcement of this rigorous law for some time to come."

It should be noted that, although rigorous in its potentialities for improved safety, the law was based on the power over commerce "among the several states, or between a place in a state and any place outside." In view of these limits on its coverage as a mandatory regulation, the law spoke of the duty "to cooperate with, and provide assistance to, the States in the development and enforcement of effective State coal mine health and safety programs. . . ." State laws with more stringent health and safety standards, if compatible, are not displaced by the national law. The realities of comprehensive control rest partly upon the adequacy of future appropriations and partly upon administrative collaboration that may include aid in the training of state inspectors. These and other factors in carrying out such laws depend heavily on executive support and administrative efficiency.[42]

The Prospects: National Regulatory
Control of Crucial Fields

By the seventies public opinion in the United States had reached the point of nearly universal acceptance in abstract terms of the need for controls on matters as fundamental as

42. Public Law 91-173, 83 Stat. 742, December 30, 1969, "Federal Coal Mine Health and Safety Act."

the quality of air and water where the swiftly mounting dangers produce consequences that may be irremediable. Beyond are human needs that are still deeper. The interests involved are disposed to temporize. Much of the legislation that they have come to accept is qualified and conditional. Many of the measures weaken the controls by dividing the responsibility in the older spirit of federalism. In many pressing matters the movement still fails to lay down prompt and mandatory requirements that provide the powers and the means for completely national control in crucial fields, if needed.

An arrangement that has begun and should spread allows for state control which goes further than the countrywide national rule. The latter continues to apply unless the state law and its administration are comprehensive and acceptable. This represents an important advance in federalism. It recognizes the need for national standards in many fields; at the same time it is an invitation to the states to act. Such situations call usually for administrative relations to help the states and local governments in administering the provisions of the law.

CONCLUSION

This chapter has shown the growing likelihood that many national laws in the future will have mandatory force over the whole of a regulatory domain, including intrastate phases. In practice this development will not displace the states that are alert and active. It will guarantee that the regulatory action is assured and comprehensive in matters where national mandatory controls are necessary. Federalism in the United States has come a long way since the nation's Attorney General ruled in 1879: "If it were known that the yellow fever at Memphis would spread only through Tennessee, the national board of health would have no power to interfere. It is only because this is not known, and because of the threat to the country, that the board can spend money in aiding state and municipal boards, etc."[43]

The United States constitution, almost unchanged since its beginning in its grant of coercively regulatory powers to the central government, was not unsound in the scanty foundation that it provided. The power to regulate interstate commerce is a basis for flexibly selective controls. The potential reach of this power, even to the length of laying down binding rules for whole fields of activity, opens wide possibilities. Only a beginning has been made in establishing the comprehensive controls that are possible under the constitution. The essence of federalism in the face of emergent problems will not only survive but also will flourish in the opportunity for energetic states, on the one hand, to push ahead with still more rigorous standards where they are appropriate and, on the other hand, to share in the controls under delegations of authority from the national government. But it should be noted in conclusion that the main point in this chapter is the nature and extent of the central government's power in its own right to deal with problems in a mandatory way.

43. *Opinions of the Attorney General,* Vol. XXVI (August 26, 1879), p. 379.

III

Growth, Taxation, Borrowing, and the Spending Power

THE FOREGOING CHAPTER has shown the basis and range of the central government's coercively regulatory powers in the United States. The present chapter surveys the fields of action where national power is less complete, although there is wide scope for support and influence. As the background the analysis will look first at the nature of interstate rivalry and at the country's uneven development. Then the central government's powers to tax, to borrow, and to dispose of its property (including the national domain) will be examined. It will be noted that the property power, important from the outset in the form of gifts of land to an individual state wherein it lay, broke new ground in 1862 by providing that all the states might lay claim to nationally owned public land, whether within their borders or not, for the establishment of colleges for education, especially in agriculture and mechanics. It will be seen, however, that before the century's end the national support was shifting from the property power, based in the national domain, to the spending power (that is, the congressional power to appropriate), supported by the nation's power to tax. Thus a revised and lasting basis was laid for the grants-in-aid that soon appeared in fields like agricultural extension and roadbuilding. Constitutional challenges at last reached the Supreme Court and were disposed of in terms that cleared the way for the proliferation of grants-in-aid with attendant choices that will be surveyed in the following chapter. But the formative issues of purpose, policy, and constitutionality are those to be treated in the paragraphs that follow.

ASPECTS OF INTERSTATE RIVALRY

Competition of sorts exists widely among the member states of a federation. Basically, of course, such rivalry is found also in unitary systems with local self-government and free enterprise. The mood is quickened by a federal structure. It gives the constituent states a larger scope for promotional or protective legislation and other forms of action. The rivalry has many forms. A few examples will show its variety. First, each member state (like self-governing areas in unitary systems) responds to forces that work to increase the amount of economic activity within its borders. It may seek to do so by keeping its standards low, avoiding high tax rates, and reducing the amount and vigor of labor union membership among the workers. In the face of such factors, states with advanced labor standards which see business moving elsewhere may become advocates of national legislation, at least temporarily. Second, related to the motive that has been mentioned is the wish to produce cheaply for foreign export. Third, and of a different sort, is the impulse to secure national legislation that protects a local product, such as the attempt of the dairy interest to discourage the use of margarine and even to bar it altogether in veterans' hospitals. A fourth example is the effort to bar goods from areas with lower costs. Fifth is the wish to keep natural resources at home, partly for local use but mainly to ensure that they will be processed in the state of origin, although not consumed there. In this field, projecting an ancient doctrine, the courts were tolerant in permitting the states to bar the export of game killed within the state. Despite this tradition, however, not a few state actions in recent years have been checked by the Supreme Court.

The protective side of the promotional impulse is likely to be especially marked in depression periods. This sort of inward turning was prominent in the decade of the thirties. Its vogue was shown in a 1937 study of interstate trade barriers.[1] A counter-attack from several sources helped to lessen it during the closing years of the decade. Nevertheless, Henry A. Wallace when Secretary of Agriculture had reason for remarking with regret that "we cannot say that we have free trade between the states."[2] In the thirties observers noted that there was a striking reversal in the American attitude toward migration and that for a time the change was a dramatic symptom of the maladjustment in our economic life.[3]

Similar rivalries do not stop even in better days economically. The variety of areal competition within the United States has been described by George F. Break.[4] "The trouble," he wrote in the sixties, "is that the state and local governments have been engaged for some time in an increasingly active competition among themselves for new business." Another writer even mentions "a New War between the States."[5] The weapons that are used include state guarantees of private loans to new businesses, direct state loans for the same purpose, local public bonds issued to finance the

1. Frederick Eugene Melder, *State and Local Barriers to Interstate Commerce in the United States: A Study in Economic Sectionalism* (Orono: University of Maine Press, 1937).

2. Henry Agard Wallace in his foreword to George R. Taylor, Edgar L. Burtis, and Frederick V. Waugh, *Barriers to Internal Trade in Farm Products* (Washington: U.S. Government Printing Office, 1939), p. iii.

3. Carter Goodrich and Associates, *Migration and Economic Opportunity* (Philadelphia: University of Pennsylvania Press, 1936).

4. George F. Break, *Intergovernmental Fiscal Relations in the United States* (Washington: The Brookings Institution, 1967), p. 23.

5. Edwin C. Gooding, *New England Bank Review,* in a four-installment analysis in October and December 1963 and July and October 1964.

building of industrial facilities for lease to private firms, tax exemptions and like concessions, and the spread of state-promoted development corporations. In the space of three years in the early sixties inducements of these sorts were offered in at least nineteen states. It was said therefore that "preferential tax treatment, for a long time almost part of the normal pattern due to the discretion exercised in the assessment of property values, is still a widely used device to attract industry."[6]

The forces at work in the rivalries of states come in part from deep-seated loyalties that include habits of residence. In contrast the economic motives for a shift in the location of industry usually care little about any one place in itself. The factors that affect the migration of capital are only partly governmental. Nevertheless, public policies, such as variations among the states in the level of relief payments, do affect the interstate movement on welfare-relief recipients. This fact is among the reasons why such systems should be national.

The ultimate geographical pattern of business and industry is not clear. In the thirties it could be said with some confidence that "The recorded changes represent for the most part not a scattering of factories up and down the length of the land, but a gradual and limited spreading and filling out of the industrial pattern within the major manufacturing regions."[7] By mid-century, partly because of a wider use of electricity in light industries, their growth, and easier transportation by road in areas that previously were almost wholly rural, manufacturing was spreading in new ways and to places that hitherto seemed consigned always to farming. The major factors are called "the three M's"—men, materials, and markets. But their interactions are subtle.

6. John E. Moes, *Local Subsidies for Industry* (Chapel Hill: The University of North Carolina Press, 1962), p. 85.
7. Daniel B. Creamer, *Is Industry Decentralizing?* (Philadelphia: The University of Pennsylvania Press, 1935), p. vii.

The filling in through the resolution of forces, so far as the pattern becomes stable, will take time.

UNEVEN DEVELOPMENT

The United States as a continental society remains unevenly developed both geographically and in the distribution of income among social groups. Equality for the South will come slowly despite its growing industrialization. It is true that the 1970 census showed that the largest gain in population among the country's four main regions had been in the South. Meanwhile, the proportion who were black, which was 33 per cent in 1900, was down to 19 per cent (largely because of migration to northern cities) as against 11 per cent for the country as a whole. During the decade of the sixties the average per capita income in the South had grown faster than in any other region. Yet at the end of the decade it was still 21 per cent below the nationwide average.

Meanwhile, a gap survives between the southern region and the other areas in wage levels. The North-South differential was nearly 100 per cent in 1907. It was down to 25 per cent in 1946. Many factors were at work in shaping and prolonging this difference. The relative absence of labor organization seemed a minor cause. A writer remarked late in the sixties: "Trade union activity, while favorable to the North, produces only about a 3 per cent difference in wage rates."[8] The reasons for the spread seem to lie in factors that are outside the normal operation of the labor market.

The foregoing facts suggest the uneven course of development in the United States. It is against this background that we must consider the role of taxation, borrowing, the disposal of public property, and the so-called spending power of Congress under the constitution. The problem has been one

8. G. W. Scully, "Interstate Wage Differentials: A Cross Section Analysis," *American Economic Review*, LIX, No. 3 (December 1969), 769.

of adjustment among the states and regions. Increasingly, however, the city neighborhoods are at a disadvantage. Even more fundamentally the main discrepancies call for equalization among groups.

TAXATION AND BORROWING

The constitution of the United States limits only indirectly the right of the states to tax and to choose the objects or activities on which they will levy their charges. Local taxation, basically, is authorized by the state constitutions or by the legislatures. An exceptional restriction in the national constitution (supplementing the commerce clause) says that "no tax or duty shall be laid on articles exported from any State." The prohibition upon the taxation of commerce is qualified in minor respects by the provision that a state may impose duties and the like that are "absolutely necessary for executing its inspection laws," and by other supplementary provisos that do not seriously modify its primary intent.

The National Government's Borrowing Power
Note has already been taken of the brief clause that follows the grant to Congress of the taxing power in the constitutional enumeration: "To borrow money on the credit of the United States." Nothing is said about the uses to which the nation's credit may be put. The purposes have ramified: they help in financing a nationwide system of local bodies for rural electrification; they help to support the building of private homes throughout the country through guarantees that aid in their financing from private sources. Some loans involve the borrowing power more directly than in the last-mentioned example. Their volume is growing. At bottom in theory, and ultimately in fact, the nation's credit and its ability to make loans on the basis of that credit is tied to the country's resources and the central government's taxing power. The credit of a powerful government like that of the

United States is such that it can be used flexibly in cutting taxes in the face of incipient recessions.[9] But we are speaking here of the use of the borrowing power. The scope seems as wide as the fields open to the nation's use of its property power and its spending power.

The Taxing Power of the Central Government
The national government's power to tax and the power to appropriate money are given in the same clause. "The Congress," says the constitution, "shall have power to lay and collect taxes, duties, imposts and excises, to pay the debts and to provide for the common defence and the general welfare of the United States. . . ." The scope of these powers was often discussed in Congress. Judicial pronouncements on the appropriating power—early named the spending power—did not come until the early twentieth century; even then (as will be noted) they dealt with the question obliquely. Remaining was the largely theoretical issue whether, even in permissive grants by the central government, a line can be drawn between those aspects of "welfare" that are "general" and those that are local. Fundamental in most of these relations is the congressional power of taxation. It calls for analysis before speaking further about the powers to borrow and to dispose of the property of the United States. Against this background we can then return to the role of the spending power as the main basis for national grants-in-aid.

The nation's power to tax is almost unlimited under the constitution. Congress has the power, noted above, to "lay and collect taxes, duties, imposts, and excises" subject to the proviso that "all duties, imposts and excises shall be uniform throughout the United States." The constitution also says that any "capitation, or other direct, tax" must be apportioned among the states on the basis of their populations.

9. George F. Break, *Federal Lending and Economic Stability* (Washington: The Brookings Institution, 1965), p. 127.

Some doubt existed about the meaning of the word "direct." During the Civil War a national income tax of sorts was levied; the Supreme Court did not challenge its constitutionality.[10] In 1895, however, the court did reject the attempt of Congress to levy a tax on individual incomes.[11] The majority members of the court held that it was direct in essence. Needless to say, apportionment in accord with state populations would be at odds with an essential principle of income taxation. After years of delay the way for a truly national income tax was opened in 1913 by the Sixteenth Amendment, which says: "The Congress shall have power to lay and collect taxes on incomes, from whatever source derived, without apportionment among the several States, and without regard to any census or enumeration." Meanwhile, a national tax on corporate incomes had been passed in 1909 and accepted on the ground that it was indirect, being a tax on the status or privilege of incorporation.

In the decades that followed something like a revolution came in the sources of the national government's revenues. No longer were tariff levies, supplemented by taxes on liquor and tobacco, the main income of the central government. The chief pillars were now the taxes on individual and corporate incomes. At mid-century the central government was getting nearly four-fifths of its tax revenues from income taxation—45.5 per cent from individuals and 33.8 per cent from the levy on corporate incomes.

All taxation has regulatory effects in some degree, although they may not be intentional. The national government began to withdraw in the early twentieth century from the use of its taxing power as a direct form of regulation. In 1922, as has been noted, the Supreme Court invalidated the attempt of Congress to prevent child labor by imposing a prohibitively high tax upon the net incomes of establishments that employed children. The court said of this new

10. *Springer* v. *United States*, 102 U.S. 586 (1880).
11. *Pollock* v. *Farmers' Loan and Trust Company*, 157 U.S. 429 (1895).

approach: "Its prohibitory and regulatory effect and purpose are palpable."[12] Almost at the same time the court blocked the attempt of Congress by taxation to prevent certain kinds of transactions in the produce exchanges that deal in farm commodities. Decisions like these had a dampening effect. In subsequent decades, however, high taxation of certain things with a hoped-for discouraging effect was upheld in the courts. Thus the Supreme Court, in accepting the constitutionality of a tax on marihuana, ruled that "The tax in question is a legitimate exercise of the taxing power despite its collateral regulatory purpose and effect."[13] Later the national objective of cleaner air helped to justify a tax on leaded gasoline. But such uses are slight in comparison with the dominant and growing use of national income taxation.

Comparative Tax Burdens

For the people of the United States as a whole, the amount paid in taxes for all purposes as a proportion of the society's national income was lower in the late sixties than in most countries of western Europe. Measured as a proportion of the gross national product, the percentage in the mid-sixties stood at 27.5 in the United States. It ranged between 28.7 and 28.9 in Denmark, Belgium, and Britain. It was 29.6 per cent in Italy and 32.9 in The Netherlands. Sweden's proportion was 37.2, with a slightly higher figure for France. Among the European countries, however, the percentage in Switzerland was considerably lower than that in the United States. Moreover, Canada's percentage at the time was slightly lower.[14]

At mid-century the national government, which early in the thirties collected considerably less than a quarter of all

---

12. *Bailey* v. *Drexel Furniture Co.*, 259 U.S. 20 at 37 (1922).
13. *United States* v. *Sanchez*, 340 U.S. 42 at 45 (1950).
14. Richard Goode, "The Tax Burden in the United States and Other Countries," *The Annals of the American Academy of Political and Social Science*, CCCLXXIX (September 1968), 85.

taxes, was taking three-quarters of all taxes paid in the United States. The remaining quarter was divided almost evenly between the states and localities. The governmental needs of these lower levels, though not always their tax yields, are fairly steady. These simple facts are a clue to the growing responsibilities of the central government and its central tax pool in the federal system of the United States. Although the bulk of the locally raised revenue came from the property tax, sales taxes were spreading among local government. Meanwhile there was justified concern about the way in which the general property tax is administered. A spokesman for the Senate Committee on Government Operations in 1970 (when this tax was yielding roughly thirty-three billion dollars) raised questions about its fairness, noting the extent to which many big business enterprises were underassessed. The question was asked whether it was consistent to allow property owners to deduct their property tax payments from the national income tax while renters did not have this privilege.

In the United States it has been customary through at least a century for the states to give aid to their local governments. Recently these transfers have amounted to more than a third of the expenditures of the state governments and to about 30 per cent of the income of the local governments. Meanwhile, the growth of national grants-in-aid to the subordinate units of government is notable. It is already large for some states. Nevertheless, in the sixties it amounted to only about 18 per cent of the combined income of the state and local governments as a whole.[15]

The early dream (as it seemed later) of a neat allocation of tax sources among the levels of government appeared in many forms during the first third of the twentieth century. Already the general property tax had been left almost entirely to local governments. In the second decade, as a phase of the recoil

---

15. Joseph A. Pechman, "Tax Policies for the 1970s," *Public Policy*, XVIII, No. 1 (Fall 1969), 84.

of the groups who saw the new national income tax as a special grievance, talk was heard of pushing back the national government; vague resolutions to that effect were passed in many state legislatures. Later and more seriously, an effort was made, even to the point of holding conferences, to negotiate an allocation of the tax sources among the levels of government. By this time many states had already entered the income tax field; eighteen together were raising thus one-tenth of their state revenues and a dozen were obtaining at least one-fifth; in only three states, however, did this source of revenue yield one-half or more of the state income from taxation of all kinds. Duplication was rife in the sense that all governmental levels were looking for sources of revenue. No direct results, however, came from the talk about an interlevel arrangement for the separation of sources. It became clear that the main way of rescuing the state and local governments must be found in the national tax pool and the nation's borrowing power.

The restrictions upon state taxation that exist, though sound from the standpoint of keeping open the national marketplace, must make terms with the ideal of cherishing the vitality of the states as members of the federal union. They and their localities must have added revenue; as taxation it is usually found (apart from levies on real property) where things are moving. Something like a dilemma has been presented to the courts in passing on the legitimacy of many forms of state and local taxation that impinges on interstate commerce. The courts, though sensitive about freedom of trade nationally, have resolved the doubt partly in favor of the right of a state to levy taxes that are nondiscriminatory in the sense that they take account of the amount of business that is done within that state. This type of problem involves one of the most tangled and troublesome issues in the law of federalism as it exists in the United States. Basically, however, the amount of state income that comes from taxation of this sort does not affect the main problems of taxation and expenditure in the federal system.

Western Germany as reconstituted under its new basic law after World War II gives lengthy and explicit attention to revenue matters in its federal constitution. Under the provisions for periodical readjustments the formula for the interlevel sharing of the income tax and the corporation tax was altered in the late fifties. The revenue clauses of the basic law provide for more interlocking and central supervision than in the United States. As to expenditures in West Germany, it is stated broadly that the central government and the Laender shall be independent of each other as regards their budgets. But the Reichstag, with the consent of the Bundesrat, can arrange for "a reasonable financial equalization between financially strong Laender and financially weak Laender." The spirit of this provision resembles the outlook that increasingly has become evident in the United States.

Some other constitutions among the newer federations give more attention than the United States to the problems of overlapping tax sources and competition for revenues among the levels of government. One answer is to vest the income tax wholly in the central government but with a provision for sharing the proceeds with the member states on a percentage basis. India is a chief example. Its solution of this aspect of a widespread problem includes the useful plan of a recurrently official but detached study of the sources and need of revenue, looking toward their periodical revision. But A. K. Chanda, former comptroller and subsequently a scholarly critic of the adequacy of India's constitutional system on several points, does not overstate things when he declares that "in no federation has it been found possible to provide for allocation of resources to correspond to allocation of functions."[16]

---

16. A. K. Chanda, "The Financial Aspect of Union-State Relations," *Journal of Constitutional and Parliamentary Studies*, III, No. 4 (October-December 1969), 137.

THE NATION'S PROPERTY POWER: THE EARLY
BASIS FOR FEDERAL AID

For a long time, almost to the end of the nineteenth century, the national government's property power was the main basis of assistance to the states and their localities. It rested upon the constitutional provision that "The Congress shall have power to dispose of and make all needful rules and regulations respecting the territory or other property belonging to the United States." The potency of this clause lay in the extent of the land area of North America (outside the original states) that was owned by the national government as a proprietor. Even today these holdings amount to half of the area that lies within the eleven western "public land" states, as they are often called. Retrospectively, it was well said by the Public Land Law Review Commission (reporting to Congress in 1970) that "one of the great ideas that marked our early public land policies was that grants of federal lands should be made to each state as it entered the union to provide a basis for its development."[17]

This policy was adopted even before the establishment of the constitution. The congressional ordinance of 1785 for the Northwest Territory, a landmark in the building of the nation, provided for rectangular surveys and the reserving of a designated lot within each township for the maintenance of public schools. The application of the policy began notably with the admission of Ohio in 1802. Altogether in the years that followed about seventy-eight million acres were granted to the entering states for the support of schools. Additional grants that totaled about one hundred and forty million acres were made to the entering states (other than Alaska) for the support of education, roads and canals, the improvement of rivers, swamp land reclamation, and miscel-

17. Report of the Public Land Law Review Commission, *One Third of the Nation's Land* (Washington: U.S. Government Printing Office, 1970), p. 243.

laneous public works. In the nineteenth century the grants of various kinds from the central government accounted for a considerable share of the income of some of the states.[18]

The support that was given was not confined to the states and their localities. The privately built railroads in the western parts of the country were empowered to lay claim to alternate tracts of land along their projected rights of way; in the aggregate these grants amounted to about one hundred and fifty million acres, equivalent to the combined area of a dozen northeastern states. Most of these grants of land, whether to public or to private recipients, were in the nature of conditional trusts that the national government might or might not care to challenge. Ordinarily it did not raise the issue in the courts. Only in later years, and then on the ground that the performance called for in the land grant had not been fulfilled, did the national government seek to reclaim some of the railroad land grants.

As early as the thirties Henry Clay had pushed through a law (vetoed by President Jackson) that proposed to distribute among the states the proceeds from the sale of public lands in proportion to their representation in Congress, provided that the funds were used by the states for internal improvements and for education. Already there was lively interest in agricultural colleges; memorials were lodged with Congress as early as the thirties. Michigan's constitution of 1850 called for an agricultural school. Pennsylvania created one four years later and in 1856 Congress authorized an investigation of the subject.

A major change in the disposal of the national domain was presaged in 1862 when President Lincoln signed a bill—the so-called Homestead Act—that had been vetoed by his predecessor. In contrast to the policy of selling public lands in large tracts, it allowed bona fide settlers to obtain without

18. Daniel J. Elazar, *The American Partnership: Intergovernmental Co-operation in the Nineteenth-Century United States* (Chicago: The University of Chicago Press, 1962).

charge up to one hundred and sixty acres of land in the public domain which they had located and had begun to improve. Almost simultaneously the President approved the bill for land grants in support of a system of state agricultural colleges,[19] thus overturning the veto of a similar bill by his predecessor.

The law of 1862, opening the public lands to all the states for the support of such agricultural colleges as they cared to establish, was not less significant because some states already had them, nor because the combined attendance of all the agricultural colleges remained small for a long time. As late as 1937 the total income of the nearly seventy "land grant" colleges then in existence was barely a million dollars from the part of their endowments that came from the location and sale of public lands.

Procedurally, as has been noted, the original law was notable in making nationally owned land available for the support of states that had no such lands within their borders. It was notable too in laying down certain conditions and in requiring annual reports. In its spirit the law was a clue to the reversal of the trend that earlier in the century had seen a decline in the proportion of young people in the United States who went to a college of any kind.

Moreover, the act of 1862 was suggestive of the ferment of humanitarian reforms in the decades of the mid-century. The work of Dorothea Lynde Dix was a sign of the times. Her interest in the care of the indigent insane had been quickened in 1840 when she began to give Sunday instruction in the Cambridge House of Correction and found insane persons in unheated rooms. Between that time and her advocacy of a national land-grant law in 1854 for aid to the states generally in caring for the indigent insane (an act killed by a presidential veto), she investigated conditions in a score of states and spoke before many legislatures in urgent

---

19. 37th Cong., Chapter 130, 12 Stat. 503, July 2, 1862.

support of hospitals to include care for insane persons. Thus the measure for the support of agricultural colleges in all the states from the proceeds of public land sales, regardless of the location of these lands, was part of a broad mood.

The launching of the nationwide plan for agricultural colleges was still an exercise of the national government's property power. The proceeds from the sale of the land was to be used in each state "for the endowment, support, and maintenance of at least one college where the leading object shall be, without excluding other scientific and classical studies, and including military tactics, to teach such branches of learning as are related to agriculture and the mechanical arts." The original program was notably supplemented by the law of 1887 (the Hatch Act) that provided for the establishment of experimental stations at the agricultural colleges. The nation's aid in the support of these stations was still in the form of a gift of land from the public domain, open to all the states. But the second step was at hand in the shift from grants of land to grants of money. A transitional amendment said that the support was to come from any money in the Treasury "arising from the sales of public lands." By the end of the century the basis was shifting squarely to the spending power. A law in 1900 authorized the Treasury to pay any deficit under the appropriation "in the event that the proceeds of the annual sale of public lands shall not be sufficient."[20] The formal divorce came finally a little later. Thereafter the spending power of Congress was the basis of federal aid.

National supervision for a long time was loose. As late as 1892 an official of the national education bureau declared that "the land grant of 1862 amounted to an absolute gift." He added: "If the institutions established did not teach agriculture or military tactics (and many of them did not do so for years), the President and his cabinet and the entire ju-

20. 56th Cong., Chapter 479, 31 Stat. 179, May 17, 1900.

diciary of the United States might whistle in the winds for redress."[21] The experiment stations, which Congress added as part of the system in the eighties, were the objects of some early complaints by national officials. The basic law of 1887 had called for an annual financial report. Later in the nineties steps were taken by Congress to make such accounting more certain. In the same year the Secretary of Agriculture, although stating that violations were few, wondered whether "it would not be best to give to this department some supervisory discretion over the expenditure of the funds granted to the stations from the national treasury."

Even in later decades there were racial inequalities that went further than the early laws permitted and that seem unpardonable in retrospect. The amending law of 1890 for the land grant colleges said that "no money shall be paid out under this act . . . for the support and maintenance of a college where a distinction of race or color is made in the admission of students, but the establishment and maintenance of such colleges separately for white and colored students shall be held to be a compliance with the provisions . . . if the funds . . . be equitably divided. . . ." As late as the third decade of the next century, when there were sixty-nine agricultural colleges, only 5.5 per cent of the land grant funds went to Negro colleges in the seventeen southern and border states although 24.9 per cent of their population was Negro.

THE SHIFT TO TAXATION AS THE BASE:
THE GROWTH OF FEDERAL AID

The systematic use of national grants-in-aid to the states and localities under the congressional spending power spread only in the early decades of the twentieth century. Mean-

21. *Proceedings of the Sixth Annual Conference of the Association of Agricultural Colleges and Experiment Stations*, p. 114.

while, the sporadic but long-existent use of assistance under appropriation acts was frequent. Thus national support was provided to states that cared to experiment in highway construction with different kinds of surfacing; New Jersey had pioneered in establishing a state highway department in the early nineties and the movement was spreading. In the agricultural field soon after the turn of the century, particularly in combating the ravages of the boll weevil in the cotton-growing areas, the national Department of Agriculture had begun a form of advisory counseling among groups of farmers that was destined to appear later and more formally as well as more fully in the system of agricultural extension.

The Burgeoning of Federal Aid

In the second decade the emerging pattern of federal aid under congressional laws took on the features that were almost standard for a score of years, although they varied a bit among the purposes in view. The basic features were: the identification of an objective; a scheme in which all states were invited to join; the authorization of the appropriation of a certain sum of money from the national treasury; an allotment to each state on the basis of a formula that was stated in the national law (often the basis was population); indication by interested states of their wish to participate in the objective (signified by a legislative enactment and including where necessary the creation of a new state department for the joint purpose); the willingness of each state (alone or with its localities) to provide annually a sum of money that would be at least as large as the national allotment; the presentation and national approval of an annual plan of action or of projects in an operation like roadbuilding; the carrying out of the plan or project by the state or its localities; incidental advice from the national government; and financial responsibility fortified by a recurrent audit. Such was the pattern that took shape in the early years of the century and that seemed to be the design as well as the essence of national grants-in-aid.

Congress in 1914 took a notable step in passing the law for agricultural extension. It provided monetary aid and some guidance for work undertaken mainly through a system of county agents. Later these were joined by home demonstration agents under the supervision of the state agricultural colleges with help from the experiment stations.[22] This statute broadened and made available to all states the kind of work that agents from the national department had helped to introduce after 1903, including the popularizing of new crops. Four years later Congress provided for federal aid to the states in developing vocational education that would help in serving both agricultural and industrial needs and training in the school systems.[23] This measure was presented in Congress as a balance in part for the financial aid that the central government was giving to agricultural extension work.

Meanwhile, in 1916 Congress had passed the landmark law that provided for federal aid in roadbuilding.[24] It required that each state in order to participate must have a state highway department. (By this time thirty-seven of the states had such departments.) Originally, the total sum that was available annually was divided among the states in proportion to population, area, and the mileage of rural postal delivery routes. From the outset a decentralizing feature was introduced at the insistence of the association of the state highway officials; it called for regional offices where the plans for construction as drawn in the states were considered.

During the country's participation in World War I Congress passed a law, designedly temporary, for aid to the state health authorities in coping with venereal disease.[25] In 1921

22. Public Law 63-95, 38 Stat. 372, May 8, 1914.
23. Public Law 64-347, 39 Stat. 929, February 23, 1917.
24. Public Law 64-156, 39 Stat. 355, July 11, 1916.
25. Public Law 65-193, 40 Stat. 845 at 886, July 9, 1918.

another law, destined soon to become controversial, offered help in maternity aid.[26] It invited the states and localities to devise ways of lessening the relatively high death rate during and after childbirth in the United States. The country's record was poor and was destined to worsen; in 1959, for example, it stood eleventh in the world in the rate of infant mortality and six years later was eighteenth. In the face of deep-seated causes and conditions the proponents of the maternity aid act did not think of it as temporary, although it was limited to a term of years. Its support in Congress was enough to have it renewed once. Nevertheless, this measure brought to a head the rising quarrel over national grants-in-aid. The maternity aid act was never accepted by Massachusetts, Connecticut, and Illinois. In part it was a fight between the urban and rural areas and in part a conflict between the larger and smaller payers of the national income tax. The lines of controversy were shaped in light of the fact that federal aid was still aimed mainly at the disadvantaged position of the rural and sparsely settled parts of the country.

The Failure of the Constitutional Attacks

The constitutional issues in the attack on the maternity aid law were decided by the Supreme Court in 1923.[27] At the time sectional rivalries in the United States were rife. Thus, on the heels of the passage of the law for federal aid in road-building, the governor of North Carolina had congratulated his people because at last it was possible to look forward to a statewide system of hard roads. In the same message, referring to the national child labor law that Congress had passed recently and before it was invalidated by the Supreme Court, he said that the conscience of the people of his state and not the "covetousness of New England" should decide about the labor laws of his state. Almost simultaneously the governor of Massachusetts spoke sarcastically about the "mud roads"

26. Public Law 67-97, 42 Stat. 224, November 23, 1921.
27. *Massachusetts* v. *Mellon* and *Frothingham* v. *Mellon,* 262 U.S. 447 (1923).

act that would extract from the people of his state six times
more than it would return as the state's allotment. But the
legislature to which he addressed this complaint passed a
resolution in favor of a national law limiting the hours of
labor for women; if necessary the constitution should be
amended to make it possible.

The lines had simplified somewhat by the time the maternity aid act was passed in 1921. The Massachusetts legislature passed a resolution that asked the attorney general to
start a lawsuit which would raise the question of its unconstitutionality in the Supreme Court. Simultaneously a taxpayer in the District of Columbia brought an action that
challenged the validity of the law.

The Supreme Court disposed of these attacks in a single
opinion. Massachusetts had no standing to sue, it said. The
state was not coerced for it was not obliged to join in the
federal aid scheme. As a state it was not involved in taxes
paid by residents in the state to the national government.
The brief in behalf of the law's constitutionality argued that
"after property has been acquired by the United States, after
funds have been brought into the Treasury and mingled
with other funds there placed, Congress has sweeping power
to dispose of these resources." The court's decision gave this
view at least glancing support. As to the remoteness of the
interest of any individual taxpayer in any particular appropriation, the decision noted that the funds in the United
States Treasury are "partly realized from taxation and partly
from other sources." This viewpoint was easier to uphold
because in the national finances generally, unlike the situation in many states and localities, specific sources of revenue
were seldom associated with specific objects of expenditure.
In the light of these arguments, the Supreme Court upheld
the maternity aid law without dealing directly with the
scope of the spending power. The practical effect of the decision seemed to leave the use of the spending power where
it had always been: within the discretion of Congress.

In the thirties the provisions of the law for agricultural relief opened the way for a different attack on the use of the spending power. An objective of the 1933 law was to raise farm prices to achieve a balance between the production and the consumption of agricultural commodities. The statute provided for payments to farmers who curtailed their planted acreage under a national plan. The scheme was constitutionally vulnerable because these payments were supported by a tax that was established by the law itself. This fact made it easier for a majority of the Supreme Court to hold that the plan was "a scheme for purchasing with federal funds submission to federal regulation of a subject reserved to the states."[28] The payments (said the opinion) were so substantial that few if any farmers could resist the impulse to take the benefits available under the law. In effect, therefore, the law was a coercively regulatory measure.

To be sure, the majority members of the court joined with the other justices in affirming the existence and validity of the national government's spending power. But the majority opinion held that under the Agricultural Adjustment Act "the amount of the tax is appropriated to be expended only in payment under contracts whereby the parties bind themselves to regulation by the federal government." On this basis the Supreme Court invalidated the 1933 law and its particular scheme for agricultural relief. The outcome was the 1938 renewal and extension of the national system for the support of agricultural prices but without the tax.

Meanwhile, constitutional doubts on several fronts were dispelled by decisions that upheld the social security act of 1934 in its several phases. These included support through the states for unemployment insurance[29] as well as the direct national system of contributory old age insurance where, said the court's decision, the problem had become "national in

28. *United States* v. *Butler,* 297 U.S. 1 at 72 and 73 (1936).
29. *Carmichael* v. *Southern Coal and Coke Company,* 301 U.S. 495 (1937), *Steward Machine Company* v. *Davis,* 301 U.S. 548 (1937).

area and dimensions." As to the question of the line between what is general and what is local in using the spending power, the Supreme Court observed that a "penumbra"
exists for the exercise of discretion. "The discretion, however, is not confided to the court," it said. Rather "the discretion belongs to Congress, unless the choice is clearly
wrong, a display of arbitrary power, not an exercise of
judgment."[30]

A possible ground for challenging the national spending
power where no coercion exists, aside from taxation and the
possibility of borrowing on the credit of the United States,
might be the argument that the financing of a public enterprise wreaks an injury on the disadvantaged or displaced
private competitors of the public activity. The answer lies
partly in the existence of competition and displacement as
features of a competitive economy. This fact does not dispose
wholly of the social grounds for concern. Constitutionally,
however, national grants and loans to public enterprises, as
in electricity, seem immune from any persuasive challenge
in the courts on the ground that their mere existence is an
improper form of competition and an abuse of the nation's
spending or borrowing powers. The Supreme Court's decisions seem to nullify such an argument.[31]

CONCLUSION

Thus the vast and tangled issues of the spending power in
the federal system of the United States, like the nation's
power to borrow and lend and to dispose of its property, remain what they have always been: political questions with
social consequences. A conservative critic could say of them
all what he called the spending power of Congress: the "vul-

---

30. *Helvering* v. *Davis*, 301 U.S. 619 at 640 (1937).

31. *Alabama Power Co.* v. *Ickes*, 302 U.S. 464 (1938), *Duke Power Co.* v. *Green-
wood County*, 302 U.S. 485 (1938), and *Tennessee Electric Power Co.* v. *Tennessee Valley Authority* (the "second TVA case"), 306 U.S. 118 (1939).

nerable heel" of an Achilles-like constitution.[32] The Supreme Court's decisions as well as the practices of Congress and the country's mood seem to have answered this critic in the end even more emphatically than when he phrased his lament in the early thirties.

At the beginning of the seventies the 24.3 million persons with incomes below the poverty line numbered fewer by fifteen million than a decade before. In the preceding year black persons and other members of minority groups accounted for slightly more than 30 per cent of the poor, although amounting to only 12 per cent of the population. The challenge of contrasts in the United States is not lessened by glaring discrepancies in the world at large. As things stand, the gap between the rich and the poor countries is widening. Infant mortality is four times higher in the poor than in the rich nations. It is said that there are a hundred million more illiterates in the world than there were a score of years ago. The gaps that exist in the United States are many, but a main one is educational, not generational. It is safe to say that there is more in common between the educated young and the educated old than between the educated young and the less-educated young. The need for further drastic compensatory and remedial action is compelling.

A double question survives. Should the national government, apart from certain mandatory controls, accomplish most of its purposes collaboratively through the state and local governments? Does the spirit of federalism, reinforced by the size of the country, point toward an indirect method of administration in many fields? The choices need not be final. Thus it is becoming increasingly desirable to shift most of the responsibility for social security to the national government, which has always administered old age insurance. Many regulatory controls, as has been said, should be-

32. James M. Beck, *Our Wonderland of Bureaucracy* (New York: Macmillan, 1932), p. 20.

come comprehensively national, although often with scope for still more drastic state standards and with an administrative devolution of responsibility upon such states as are interested and active. In partial contrast, it is the multiplying services of government that are the essence of the growing system of grants-in-aid. Their nature today and in the future is the theme of the chapter that follows.

IV

The Maturing of Grants-in-Aid

THE SCOPE OF THE SPENDING POWER of Congress often leaves a major choice for statecraft in the United States. Should the national government act wholly through its own administrative facilities or should it accomplish its purpose through the states and localities in conducting programs which, being permissive, involve inducements but do not depend upon penalties? The choice is not an outright one. It is a question of emphasis that, already weighty, is likely to grow in its range and importance.

Often the programs that the central government helps to support through grants-in-aid require the incidental use of regulatory powers that are possessed only by the states and their local governments. Limits have been placed, for example, on the national government's ability to acquire private property by condemnation. In 1935 the Court of Appeals held that the national government did not have the power to acquire land that the owners were unwilling to sell but that was needed for a public housing project in Louisville.[1] The government did not appeal the case; it abandoned the particular housing project and soon shifted to the indirect method of promoting public housing by giv-

1. *United States* v. *Certain Lands in the City of Louisville,* 78 F 2nd 684 (1935).

ing aid to housing authorities organized under state and local laws. Doubtless in more recent years the scope of the national government's direct use of condemnation has broadened. Such was the implication of the Supreme Court's decision in 1946 that allowed the Tennessee Valley Authority to acquire property by condemnation in rearranging the use of lands around one of its reservoirs.

But even with the progressive broadening of the national government's right to acquire property directly for purposes that are not regulatory, many other grounds exist for acting through the state and local governments. These reasons do not lie solely or even mainly in the fact that often there is need for the use of powers possessed only by the state governments. The deeper reasons lie in the spirit of the federal system and the scope it gives for dispersing judgment as well as details. It invites the localizing of these matters even when a general plan and much of the money come from the national government.

Testifying in 1966 before the Senate Committee on Government Operations, the then Director of the Budget, Charles L. Schultze, mentioned that the preceding Congress had enacted twenty-one new health programs, seventeen new educational programs, fifteen new economic development programs, twelve new programs to meet city problems, four new programs for manpower training, and seventeen new resource development programs. These, he said, could have been shaped as direct operations of the central government, thus avoiding some difficult intergovernmental problems. But this course "would not have led to effective solutions, since most of the problems which these programs attack are not the same nation-wide, and can only be solved in the context of widely different local conditions and requirements." The soundness of this outlook is not denied by the fact that many national programs, when conducted wisely and with skill, can provide a good deal of experimenting and adaptation. On the whole, however, the case for acting indi-

rectly through a variety of grants-in-aid is strengthened by
the wholesomeness of local and regional variations as well as
the frequent need for the collateral use of state governmental powers.

THE RELATIVE SHIFT TO URBAN PROBLEMS

In the United States for many decades the stress in both federal and state aid was on supplementary assistance to the
countryside, which was beset by the cost of services in
sparsely settled areas. The emphasis in England's use of
grants-in-aid was almost the reverse; that country's pattern
was a harbinger of the shift to urban needs that would come
later in the United States. Yet the institutions of both countries ran parallel in responding to needs that were deeper
than constitutional forms. In England, where unitary government is combined with a tradition of locally elected
bodies, Sidney Webb ventured to suggest in 1911 "that the
Grant in Aid, mere financial adjustment though it seems to
be, is more and more becoming the pivot on which the machine really works."[2]

The reasons mentioned for national grants-in-aid to localities included the need for mitigation of the inequalities that
have a marked relation to (a) the number of children, (b)
the degree of sickness, (c) premature invalidity, (d) the
amount of traffic, (e) the conditions of housing, and (f) the
relative poverty of the population. In addition, as things
stood in England at the beginning of the second decade of
the century (seventy-five years after the beginnings of the
system), a national system of grants-in-aid was needed to secure effective authority for the necessary supervision and
control by the central government, to encourage the kinds of
expenditure that were most desirable for the communities,
and to make it possible to attain anything like the "national

2. Sidney Webb, *Grants in Aid: A Criticism and a Proposal* (London: Long-
mans, Green, 1911), p. 3.

minimum" that Parliament had set as a goal. Even in the United States later in the century many of these problems and objectives continue to underlie the case for grants-in-aid, partly in the older systems of state aid to localities but increasingly in federal aid to the states and their subdivisions.

After 1933, when federal aid in the United States burgeoned in ever more novel forms, it aimed increasingly at problems of congestion, poverty, and the conditions of interdependent living. It had become a customary device in nation-state-local relations for the separate handling of diverse social objectives, related by something of a common mood. Political victories had confirmed its standing despite some continued grumbling. But even the complainants granted the necessity of financial aid from the central treasury. The controversy was shifting to the form of the aid.

THE ISSUES IN FEDERAL AID AT MID-CENTURY AND AFTER

The flow of financial support from the larger to the smaller units of government presents a cluster of problems. They center in the specialized nature of interlevel grants. Thus far in the United States federal aid has been mostly for the stimulation and support of specified purposes. This principle, beginning as early as the seventies in the last century, was an outstanding feature of the state grants to help localities in supporting schools and, subsequently, other functions. Federal aid followed this course in stressing particular objectives. The maturing of the system deepens problems concerning its effects on the participating governments. Is the administrative coherence in the national government hurt by the scattered nature of the grants-in-aid? Is similar harm done at the levels that receive this aid? Does the solution lie in broadening the categories? Would government in the states and localities be more coherent, as well as more self-reliant, if the national financial assistance was given unconditionally? Is there a middle-ground solution by which the conditional forms of aid would be retained but with broadened categories, while additional aid would be given unconditionally? A further problem attends the use of unconditional grants: how to make sure that they will be fairly distributed between the state government and the cities and other local units within the state.

A second main cluster of issues involves the basis of apportionment. Federal aid originally used some common measure, such as the respective populations of the states. The measure fixed the maximum amount that each state could receive if it cared to join the cooperative scheme. It was customary in addition to require the appropriation by each state of a sum of money that was at least equal to the sum provided by the national government. A major development in national grants-in-aid since the mid-forties has been the use of a ratio that is adjusted in terms of the differences in per capita wealth from state to state. The schemes themselves remained universal in their coverage: they were open to all the states. The late Senator Robert Taft, who had come to accept the equalizing role of federal aid but was conservatively minded, failed in his wish to confine federal aid to the especially needful states. Today and for the future, what should be the role of per capita wealth among states and localities and also among individual families in fixing the amount of federal aid to which each state is entitled?

A third series of problems in the maturing of grants-in-aid has to do with economic fluctuations. What should be the counter-cyclical strategies? It seems clear that they must be different for the central government and for the states and localities. In times of depression should not the volume of the grants to the states not only continue but even increase, considering the national government's flexibility in borrowing? Such a policy is supported by cogent arguments. The needs of the local units of government are fairly heavy; they can hardly curtail their spending in economic downturns. Some of their costs increase as additional burdens fall on them. The variations must be handled by the larger units, especially the central government. Agencies that look ahead have been experimenting for decades with planning for public works that can be put into fuller operation during downswings of the business cycle. Most of the foregoing and like adjustments are accepted nowadays as features of a modern fiscal policy. The unanswered issues are largely in the methods. The needed inventions may profoundly affect both interlevel relations and the administration of grants-in-aid. Increasingly, federal aid laws, in varying language, seek reasonable assurance that the grants will not result in any decrease in the level of state, local, or other non-federal funds.[3]

A fourth kind of issue is involved in relaxing the traditional requirement for matching the nation's contribution. It has been noted that the "fifty-fifty" rule is departed from in federal aid schemes that vary the proportion of the nation's share on the basis of differences in per capita wealth among the states. How important is matching in the emergent uses of federal aid? Among the hundreds of laws for national aid to states and localities, the requirements for action on the lower levels vary widely. In some cases the central government assumes the whole cost. Often this is done for stimulative and temporary purposes. Increasingly, however, the objectives of national support aim at long-run problems.

A fifth cluster of questions arises from the fact that, although interstate differences in average per capita wealth are important, the variations that exist locally and between groups within the states are also significant. Numerous examples are at hand of programs for chronically disadvantaged areas. These (like Appalachia) may involve parts of many states. How should federal aid adjust itself in seeking to cope with this sort of spotty situation?

By mid-century the uses of grants-in-aid in the United

3. An example was Public Law 91-517, 84 Stat. 1316, October 30, 1970, "Developmental Disabilities Services and Facilities Construction Act."

States had already overflowed the almost standardized channel they followed when their range and substance were analyzed by Jane Perry Clark.[4] New dimensions were appearing. These were summarized in the late sixties by the national budget director. In many programs the central government "directly participates in specific projects in states and communities" and "acts as a co-equal partner with state and local governments in carrying out these projects." In some the nation "works with a number of local governments organized into special groups." These developments had already brought new administrative problems, since such programs usually require action by several national agencies rather than by a single one as had been the case in the early grants-in-aid schemes. An attendant feature is the fact that the emerging programs can not depend upon clear lines of authority from superior to subordinate. Rather they "place a high premium on close cooperation and a steady flow of information among equals." An accompanying trend is the shifting of operating decisions into the field.

The standards of division were flexible in many of the later laws, leaving much to the discretion of national agencies. An example was the 1969 law that amended a so-called economic opportunity act. The director was empowered to establish criteria for achieving an equitable distribution of assistance among the states. In developing such criteria, said the law, "he shall consider, among other relevant factors, the ratios of population, unemployment, and family income levels." A limit was set, however: no more than 12.5 per cent could be used within any state in any fiscal year.

Many of the older landmarks of federal aid survive, but as the waters rise they spread variously in hundreds of channels. Many of the relationships are with particular states and localities. Whether targeted in this way or open to all parts of the country, the emphasis is still upon the cooperative ad-

4. Jane Perry Clark, *The Rise of a New Federalism: Federal-State Cooperation in the United States* (New York: Columbia University Press, 1938).

ministration of permissive services at a time when these are multiplying. Federal aid laws in 1946 and after did begin to provide for the possibility of lawsuits by the states if their grants were withheld or withdrawn. Meanwhile, the functions of government were growing. The constitutional arrangement and the spirit of federalism itself, as has been said, cause much of the work to flow through the states and localities. As an earlier chapter has noted, national-state-local relations in the United States began increasingly to take on some of the features of what has been called indirect federal administration in other systems. This trend deepens the collaboration among the levels of government in the United States.

THE MOUNTING VOLUME AND VARIETY OF GRANTS-IN-AID

The proliferating of federal aid came mainly after the middle of the century. Beginning in 1960, the types of aid tended to shift toward a still more active involvement of the national government in many new fields. A growing number of the fresh programs dealt directly with the local governments. As many as twenty-three of the thirty-eight federal aid laws passed after 1960 bypassed the states. The total volume of federal aid to the states and localities expanded rapidly. As late as 1958 they amounted to slightly less than five billion dollars. They had reached twenty-five billion dollars at the beginning of the seventies. This total (already a sizable share of the national government's yearly appropriations, if defense in all its phases is excluded) amounted to 18 per cent of the combined income of the state and local governments. The proportion varied among the states. In Arkansas, for example, the national contribution in the seventies was over one-third of the intake of the state and local governments.

For the country as a whole a forecast for the fiscal year 1972 put the total of federal aid to states and localities at thirty-nine billion dollars (up from seven billions in 1960), which amounted to 16.7 per cent of the total outlays of the national government and 26.5 per cent of its domestic outlays. As a percentage of the combined revenues of state and local governments the federal aid would be 22.4 per cent as against 12.7 in 1960. Meanwhile, the requirement for the "matching" of the national contribution had relaxed. Far from the fifty-fifty matching requirement which earlier had prevailed widely, in 1966, for example, the state and local governments provided 5.5 billion dollars of their own funds as against 13 billion dollars of national grants in that year.

It is not easy to say how many separate programs are involved. The tendency (as noted) has been for the national government to provide aid for specific purposes. Many are so closely related that in some counts they are treated as a single program. A rough total will suffice to show the proliferation. About 40 per cent of the federal aid programs were added from 1961 to 1968. At the end of that decade (according to one method of counting) about four hundred schemes of federal aid existed under national laws.[5] These were in addition to directly operated national activities in fields like flood control, national parks, and watershed protection. The crescendo of federal aid led some sympathetic commentators to speak of "program indigestion." Basically, as the late Gerhard Colm remarked, the problem of proliferation was qualitative rather than quantitative. Many of the programs were overlapping and partly inconsistent. The consolidation of programs, along with the question of local discretion, was not a new issue, but conditions were bringing it to a head. The issues merged in the problems of supervision.

In the late sixties, reporting the measure that became the Intergovernmental Cooperation Act, a House committee noted that the four hundred federal grants-in-aid programs in operation were administered by eighteen national depart-

5. Charles L. Schultze (ed.), *Agenda for the Nation* (Washington, D.C.: The Brookings Institution, 1969), p. 35, in the editor's own essay on "Budget Alternatives After Vietnam."

ments and cost nationally more than twenty billion dollars a year.[6] The measure was presented as a "responsible first step" in strengthening the state and local governments and smoothing their interaction with the central authorities. The report admitted that many difficulties would remain in the field of interstate relations.

METHODS OF SUPERVISION

Supervision in the right degree and style under conditional forms of federal aid helps the vitality of the state and local units. It was said by V. O. Key, Jr. that "the federal-aid system strengthens the states and thereby strengthens but profoundly modifies the federal system."[7] This verdict seems no less sound today because it was voiced before the recent multiplying of novel forms of interlevel collaboration. The role of the central headquarters in a collaborative system is indispensable in many ways. It includes the research that individual states and localities could not do by themselves or would do only at the cost of much duplication. It goes beyond the valuable contribution of the central government as a clearing house of experience. It provides the guiding norms that, fusing the national and the local objectives, afford a flexible basis for regional supervision.

But the foregoing assumptions about the role of supervision, though sound from the present author's point of view, are debatable as viewed by many persons. Probably most observers would agree that the standards should be those of performance or achievement, rather than providing the exact structures or procedures by which the results are to be accomplished. The supervisory routines differ from the omnibus programs that cover a year's activities on the one

---

6. 90th Cong., 2nd Session, House Report No. 1845, August 2, 1968, p. 9.
7. V. O. Key, Jr., *The Administration of Federal Grants to States* (Chicago: Public Administration Service, 1937), p. 375.

hand to the separate submission and approval of individual projects on the other. In federal aid generally the approval of an annual plan or of projects is followed by some type of national inspection. A periodical report is a third phase of the routines of control. Audit of some kind is the final stage in the rotational operation of a continuing process. These steps are durably sound in their essentials.

A step toward control that was also liberating was taken by the Intergovernmental Cooperation Act of 1968.[8] Especially in point are the provisions to improve the conduct of grants-in-aid. The new rules seek to give added leeway for the handling of programs at the state level. The governor is to be kept fully informed. Money received from the national government need not be held in a special account. The transfer of funds is to be so scheduled that it will minimize the time between the transfer from the United States Treasury and disbursement in the state. Moreover, at the governor's request, the national government may waive the arrangements for the conduct of a program by either a single agency or a multimember board if it is shown that the provision in question prevents an efficient arrangement within the state government. In addition to the objective of more flexibility at the state level, the law directs the President to "establish rules and regulations governing the formulation, evaluation, and review of Federal programs and projects having a significant impact on area and community development, including programs providing for Federal assistance to the States and localities." The law says further that federal aid for development purposes must be consistent with and help in advancing the objectives of state, regional, and local planning of a comprehensive sort.

The Intergovernmental Cooperation Act does not provide for an automatic termination of national laws for grants-in-aid after a certain length of time. Such a provision was wisely

8. Public Law 90-577, 82 Stat. 1098, October 16, 1968.

dropped, although it had been proposed by many critics of federal aid. The law does say that if no terminal date is stated in a law, an inquiry must be made before the end of the fourth year by the congressional committee with jurisdiction over the subject matter of the grant in question. The committee's report to Congress after this review (possibly supplemented by a comment from the Comptroller General) will analyze the extent to which the law's purpose has been fulfilled, whether the objective in view can be carried on without further financial assistance from the national government, whether there should be shift of emphasis, and whether the amount of money provided is adequate in view of the need. The provisions mentioned were colored in part by the assumption that many of the schemes were stimulative and intended to be temporary.

Nevertheless, the call for a recurrent appraisal did recognize that a new and lasting stage had come in the interlevel distribution of the nation's taxable resources as well as the interlevel sharing of purposes and ideas. A typical statement said: "withholding of funds is the remedy prescribed by law for noncompliance." On this basis a warning was issued to two states under the program for aid to families with dependent children. It was noted that in the past only one state had irrevocably lost national grants-in-aid for alleged violations of the welfare rules.

Sparse use has been made administratively of the "sanctions" that exist under federal aid. The national viewpoint that discourages resort to discipline was voiced by the director: "It is a step we take with great reluctance because of its potentially serious impact on needy families." Usually action goes no further than cutting off the funds (or part of them), though sometimes the statutes allow the national government to ask for a refund. In practice, the national federal aid officials are likely to share the outlook that the late Harry Hopkins, when in charge of welfare aid during the depression in the thirties, confessed was his repentant thought after cutting off the funds for Ohio because of certain actions on the part of the governor of that state. After all, concluded Hopkins, it was he who had lost the battle. His objective was to help the needy people of Ohio, not to win in a conflict over rules and procedures with the governor. The national government's use of its controls, whether in the withholding of funds or otherwise, has been slight in comparison with the totality of relations that are involved in grants-in-aid. But it became customary to include a provision under which a state government could resort to the courts in challenging the nation's action in such procedures as the cutting off of aid.

EQUALIZING THE GRANTS IN TERMS OF INCOME LEVELS

Grants-in-aid to the states from the outset took account of population as a measure of need, but failed to reckon with variations in per capita income. After World War II the system began to take account of this factor. The principle called equalization was introduced, and many of the formulas for the distribution of federal aid among the states were modified accordingly. Whereas the original idea had been merely to match the state's contribution while encouraging the state to spend more for the objective in view, under the newer schemes the states with lower per capita income received a larger national contribution on the basis of a sliding scale. Crudely at least this affirmed and made operative the wish that was expressed through Congress to shape federal aid still further as an equalizing device.

A step still to be taken may come when the statistical means are perfected and applied for comparing the relative "sacrifice" made by each of the states and localities under its tax system. Much study has been given to this question.[9]

9. The Advisory Commission on Intergovernmental Relations, *Measures of State and Local Fiscal Capacity and Tax Effort: A Staff Report,* October 1962.

A possible method of measurement is to compare the yields of existing taxes, as a percentage of a people's income, with the proportional amount that would be raised in each state under a model tax system. This would throw light on the existing degree of sacrifice in each part of the country. It would provide a guide both for the reshaping of state and local tax systems and for the redistribution of wealth through grants-in-aid. It is in point to add that at mid-century the record of the southern states showed that in general they were taxing themselves at least as heavily as other parts of the country and more heavily than some. In the future, federal aid may learn to take account of the relative tax burdens among the states.

Looking to the decades ahead, one can hardly foresee the time when the geographical distribution of taxable wealth will coincide with that of people and their needs. We refer here to variations among the states, not to the still greater variations among families and neighborhoods. It is fortunate that in the United States the gaps are closing among the major regions. In 1880, in terms of the national average of per capita income, the country's highest region stood at 211 per cent, the lowest at 50 per cent; in 1957 they were 119 per cent and 70 per cent, respectively.[10] The lifting and leveling processes at work in the country's economy are sometimes dramatic, notably in the per capita advance of the southern states, although not among all groups. But the over-all progress is slow as measured by the index of statewide per capita income levels. Mississippi in recent times has had one of the highest rates in the growth of statewide per capita income; the increase was three times greater than that of Connecticut. But even in the sixties the per capita income in Connecticut was double that in Mississippi. Persistent discrepancies of this kind were among the factors that

10. Harvey S. Perloff, Edgar S. Dunn, Jr., Eric E. Lampard, and Richard F. Muth, *Regions, Resources, and Economic Growth* (Baltimore: The Johns Hopkins Press, 1960), p. 25.

led Congress to modify the "matching" principle in federal aid.

In accepting the principle of equalization as one of the objectives that underlie national grants-in-aid, Congress has wisely declined to confine the aid to states that are below a certain per capita level of wealth. Equalization is not the sole purpose for the transfer of money to the state and local governments. The programs generally, pursuing national objectives that have local aspects, profit by the participation of all the states. Especially is the resilience of the collaborative system helped by the presence of the active and expressive state and local governments. This fact, however, should not be a bar either to wider adoption of the sliding scale that has been described or to the growing practice of identifying and dealing nationally with particular regions and localities in point of their distinctive needs, their possibilities, and their alertness.

A growing proportion of the methods of assisting and acting through the state and local governments are departing from the pattern that was familiar earlier in the century. To be sure, many of its laws and its basic outlines survive and will continue. But new features are appearing. They go beyond the important advance in the equalizing role of national grants-in-aid that has been discussed. Some stimulative grants, as in planning, provide nearly the whole (sometimes indeed all) of the exploratory costs. Many of the collaborative projects are confined to identified areas. Nevertheless, whether open to all the states or limited to particular places, the aid is targeted in point of its objective. In this crucial respect it remains conditional.

BROADENING THE CATEGORIES OF FEDERAL AID

The future course for the United States should be to broaden the categories of aid rather than to move completely or even primarily to a system of unconditional grants. Harold Seidman says truly that the profusion of categories and subcategories of federal grants has probably been the single most important source of management and coordination problems. Basically, however, the conditioning of the system of national grants to the states and their subdivisions preserves financial responsibility. Even more important is the administrative linkage between the governmental levels. A center and a challenge in broad fields of activity would be useful, even if all good ideas arose in the state and local domains. The national headquarters helps to spread the benefits of invention. It is doubly creative: it contributes something of its own while it acts as a clearing point in broadening a program. These assets are not lost and others are gained when the functional fields are retained but broadened. The wholesome result is more leeway at lower levels, nearer to the work itself.

Stages in Applying the Policy

It is encouraging to note the steps that are being taken along this line. The President's budget message in 1967 mentioned the beginnings in the previous year of "a new partnership in health programs through which numerous separate grant programs are being brought together." He referred to "the Partnership in Health Act of 1966," which had brought together a number of separate and small grants-in-aid; it aimed at public health services that would be more comprehensive. This law was the first sign of congressional support for the idea of grant consolidation. The Council of Economic Advisers cited the example as an indication of the possibility of further broadening and combining the scope of many federal grants. The budget message promised that other areas of federal aid would be examined "to determine whether additional categorical grants can be combined to form a more effective tool for intergovernmental cooperation."

The federal aid program for Model Cities was a step toward grant consolidation. The grants were used locally for things as varied as hiring extra personnel in the schools and building hospitals. Further moves at the time toward unification in other fields did meet with resistance. Much of this resulted from the zeal along with bureaucratic self-interest that accompany needful services. The specialization of objectives may be needed in the pioneering stages. A commentator observed that "block grants for purposes as broad as getting rid of poverty, for example; will be relatively ineffective in states which are not terribly interested in getting rid of poverty—and these are by and large the poorest states."[11]

In 1969 a message from President Nixon asked Congress to pass a grant consolidation act. It would allow the chief executive to initiate the merger of closely related federal assistance programs, subject to veto by either chamber. The proposal was confined to closely related functional areas. It took account of the diversities among the sliding scales that have been mentioned. "Thus," said the message, "if a program providing for a 10 per cent State matching share were being merged with one providing a 20 per cent matching share" the proposed plan must provide "a matching share between 10 and 20 per cent." Altogether the presidential message was forward-looking in picturing the grant consolidation proposal as "another vital step" in the administrative reforms undertaken already, such as establishing common regional boundaries for federal agencies, creating the Urban Affairs Council and the Office of Intergovernmental Relations, and beginning "a streamlining of administrative procedures for Federal grants-in-aid programs."

Such consolidations are essential in the maturing of federal aid to state and local governments. But the advance is likely to come in stages. At the outset in any forward movement the central government's role, being stimulative as well as financially supportive, tends to stress certain objectives and

11. Robert A. Levine, "Rethinking Our Social Strategies," *The Public Interest*, No. 10 (Winter 1968), 87.

particular points of need. Later a consolidating stage may be appropriate with less segregation of funds and still more leeway for state and local governments. The long-run development of national aid to education may follow this sequence. In the sixties it appeared, after small and scattered beginnings, as one of the chief domains of federal aid. As a new field, aiming at particular needs and inequalities as well as collateral support, the several billions of dollars that were provided by the Congress were made available for specified purposes. Simultaneously, the central government was beginning to extend aid to higher education. It is instructive to note the rise and initial nature of these momentous though belated additions to national grants-in-aid, especially in helping to support the elementary and secondary schools with explicit attention to the heritages of poverty.

This aid to general education may truly be called belated. Congress after the Civil War was shortsighted in failing to pass the law for national financial help to schools throughout the country that was pushed notably by Senator George F. Hoar. If it had been enacted and adequately supported, it would have lessened a century-long tragedy. National action was overdue in 1938 when an advisory commission on education recommended the establishment by Congress of a national system of grants-in-aid for schools. But twenty-seven years passed before federal aid for the primary and secondary schools and for higher education was provided under the series of laws that were launched in the middle sixties.

Illustrative Applications of the Policy

The educational needs of children in low-income families also were recognized in a series of significant enactments that began in 1965. In the first of these Congress declared it to be "the policy of the United States to provide financial assistance . . . to local educational agencies serving areas with concentrations of children from low-income families" and to improve their educational methods "by various means which contribute particularly to meeting the special educational needs of educationally deprived children." One of the titles of this law dealt with grants for supplementary educational centers and services, to stimulate and assist in the provision of vitally needed educational services not available in sufficient quantity or quality, and to stimulate and assist in the development and establishment of exemplary elementary and secondary school educational programs to serve as models for regular school programs.[12]

This series of laws provided a formula for the distribution of funds among the states and also principles for the guidance of the chief educational officer of each state. The 1970 statute sought to reduce the risk that the national grants might lessen state and local appropriations by providing that the federal funds should "supplement and, to the extent possible, increase the level of funds that would, in the absence of such federal funds, be made available from non-federal sources."[13] On the matter of desegregation this law also called for uniformity in all regions regardless of what may have been the original causes of the segregation.

A similar selectivity in point of needs was present in the series of federal aid laws for institutions of higher education. The statute of 1965 spoke of the wish to help developing institutions "which for financial and other reasons are struggling for survival and are isolated from the main currents of academic life."[14] Amendments in 1967 stressed the training of teachers, saying that a purpose of the act was "to coordinate, broaden, and strengthen programs for the training and improvement of the qualifications of teachers and other educational personnel for all levels of the American educational system. . . ."[15] In general, the relationships, whether by

12. Public Law 89-10, 79 Stat. 27, April 11, 1965, "Elementary and Secondary Education Act."
13. Public Law 91-230, 84 Stat. 121, April 13, 1970.
14. Public Law 89-329, 79 Stat. 1219, November 8, 1965, "The Higher Education Act of 1965."
15. Public Law 90-35, 81 Stat. 81, June 29, 1967.

grants or by contracts, called for consultation with the state educational authorities. Soon after, Congress requested a presidential report on the "feasibility of making available a post-secondary education to all young Americans who qualify and seek it."[16]

The foregoing examples are enough to show the pointed objectives that were stressed in the national aid to general and higher education in the late sixties. At the end of that decade money was going to about two-thirds of the country's twenty thousand school districts. Nevertheless, the total national grants were meeting only about 8 per cent of the educational costs. In the decade of the seventies it was guessed that the national share might rise to 25 or 30 per cent. It has been noted that, in the manner of federal aid generally, the early objectives struck at particular points of need and opportunity. In the future it is likely that the aid will not only increase but also broaden. This trend will include the merging of many grants with stress upon leeway in supervisory regions, states, and localities.

The variety of federal aid affords a rich opportunity for constructive mergers of function within main fields, supplemented by arrangements for flexibility in the transfer of funds and attended by the easing of many prescriptive details. Doubtless in future decades this process will advance by stages in the sense that certain novel ideas will develop first through isolated grants, to be absorbed later in the broader programs. Mostly, however, the major purposes will become stabilized with room for organic additions. The progressive amalgamations will be wholesome when the flexibility they give is accompanied by the will and means for planning at all levels. But the creative impulse that is embodied in certain essential national standards (like desegregation as a condition of aid) would be frustrated without such standards.

16. Public Law 90-575, 82 Stat. 1014, October 16, 1968.

UNCONDITIONAL GRANTS: A SUPPLEMENT
BUT NOT A SUBSTITUTE

Wholly different from a complete supplanting of conditional grants is the collateral use of an unconditional grant to help in supporting state and local governments. This idea got attention and prestige when it was broached in 1964 by Walter W. Heller, then chairman of the Council of Economic Advisers. It was endorsed by a presidential advisory group and at the time seemed to be supported by the President himself. The advocates of this proposal did not assume that it would supplant the older system. "Conditional grants for specific functions," declared Professor Heller in public lectures after returning to his university, "play an indispensable role in our federalism."[17] The original plan was to pay into a trust fund each year a specified percentage of the income tax yield (perhaps 1 or 2 per cent) which would be distributed to the states in proportion to their respective populations. No strings would be attached.

The arguments in favor of an untied type of grant, taking shape in a time of relative ease in the national financial situation, emphasize first the personal and corporate forms of income taxation available to the central government. The advocates point to the growing disadvantages that attend the inelastic and mostly regressive state and local tax systems. They point also to the foreseeable consequence from the growth of populations and from servicing needs that would add to the already heavy local tasks. These conditions are cited in favor of a supplementary use of the central government's uniquely advantaged power to tax. A system of unconditional grants could draw on this source without increasing the national government's influence upon public policy at the lower levels.

17. Walter W. Heller, *New Dimensions of Political Economy* (Cambridge, Mass.: Harvard University Press, 1966), p. 141, in a chapter on "Strengthening the Fiscal Base of our Federalism."

It is true that the idea of a wholly unconditional system of national grants-in-aid has some advocates. They can point to other federal systems, most of them in countries where the central government has larger taxing scope: perhaps with an exclusively national income tax, as in India. In the United States the persons who imagine a wholesale change in the fiscal relations of national and state governments with a system of wholly unconditional grants are likely to be those who, though they have come to accept the inevitability of drawing on the national tax pool, wish to minimize the influence of the central government upon issues of policy. This phase of the argument is seldom voiced openly. The counter-arguments are formidable apart from the difficulty of a major change in federal relations. Such a scheme would increase the risks of irresponsibility in the use of the transferred funds. It would give up the advantages that lie in the circularity of ideas that is helped by conditional forms of aid. Moreover, a system of wholly unconditional payments would jeopardize the flow of funds to local governments unless this miscarriage was guarded against by restrictions that would compromise the supposed simplicity of a scheme of unconditional grants. The adoption of such an arrangement seems unlikely in the United States.

A persuasive case exists, however, for a large though supplementary use of unconditional grants. It might lessen the competition among the states and localities which, in their effort to attract business, may shortsightedly discourage the use of taxing powers even in the wealthiest jurisdictions. A system of unconditional grants would help the poorer states and local governments to improve their public services.[18] A difficulty to be overcome would be the risk that unconditional federal grants (perhaps to a greater extent than conditional forms of aid) would provide an excuse for lowering state and local tax rates rather than expanding the services

18. George F. Break, *Intergovernmental Fiscal Relations in the United States* (Washington, D.C.: The Brookings Institution, 1967), p. 242.

that are needed.[19] In short, the case for unconditional grants (as part of a complex that includes conditional aid) is persuasive but not without difficulties. A troublesome question, in addition to the problem of dividing the national grant among the states on some fair and constructive basis, is the way in which it should be shared between each state government and its localities.

A possible combination of conditional and unconditional subsidies was recommended by the Advisory Commission on Intergovernmental Relations in 1967.[20] The system would combine categorical grants-in-aid with functional block grants of more general scope and would introduce per capita payments in support of the lower units of government. "Each of these mechanisms" said the commission, "is designed to, and should be used to, meet the categorical grant-in-aid to stimulate and support programs in specific areas of national interest and promote experimentation and demonstration in such areas; block grants, through the consolidation of existing specific grants-in-aid, to give states and localities greater flexibility in meeting needs in broad functional areas; and general support payments on a per capita basis, adjusted for variations in tax effort, to allow states and localities to devise their own programs and set their own priorities in helping to solve their unique and most critical problems."

Wide leeway for municipal governments under national aid, approximating the practice of unconditional grants, gathered strength in the latter half of the sixties. The initial step taken in the middle of that decade seemed fruitful in winning at least a foothold for the participation of poor people. The program for model cities that soon emerged (whatever may be its long-run scope and future name) passed through a period

19. Harvey S. Perloff and Richard P. Nathan (eds.), *Revenue Sharing and the City* (Baltimore: The Johns Hopkins Press, 1968).
20. Advisory Commission on Intergovernmental Relations, *Fiscal Balance in the American Federal System—A Commission Report* (Washington, D.C.: U.S. Government Printing Office, 1967), Vol. 1, p. xxi.

of trial. Basically, however, it pointed to a durable program with the possibility of local choices of emphasis among the things to be done.

CONCLUSION

The future course for the United States points to a progressive consolidation of conditional grants-in-aid, with a supplementary use of unconditional grants. Both will help by sharing with the state and local governments a part of the yield of the national income tax, with resort to national borrowing available as an aid in smoothing out such irregularities as persist in the business cycle. The combined system of sharing national taxes must make sure that the states and localities tax themselves evenly in terms of their resources; malingering on the part of some states would undermine the equity of the system as a whole. Moreover, any future scheme must guarantee that support from the central government, unconditional as well as conditional, is shared equitably within each state between the state government and the urban and other local governments and also among the latter. It is likely to remain true that, in the words of the Advisory Commission on Intergovernmental Relations, "'The federal government can assemble expertise that individual communities cannot hope to match." The growing importance of these issues will be shown further in the two following chapters.

V

Changing Roles for the States

IT IS SAID TRULY that governance in a federalism like the United States is a triangle that involves the activities of the nation, the states, and the localities. Help and guidance of many kinds now flow from the country's central government to the other partners. Weapons aside, it is nevertheless the latter that do most of the work. In 1971, 78 per cent of governmental civilian employment as a whole was in the states and localities. Especially meaningful was the fact that the number of national employees had been nearly steady for three decades, whereas the combined total of state and local governmental employees had tripled, growing from about three million to more than ten million. These facts are enough to show the combined role of state and local activities. The proportion is not likely to be affected by the future growth of federal aid from the nation's tax pool.

The figures that have been given are for the local and state governments together. The annual outlays of the two levels are about equal. An important question in the evolution of the federal system is the extent to which each level will receive grants directly from the central government. This is likely to be a major issue in the country's politics for many decades. Already there have been signs that conservative opinion (reconciled now to the fact of support from the national tax pool) may be tempted to increase the vesting of national grants-in-aid in the state governments, at least so long as state legislatures are influenced by the voting power in relatively wealthy suburban municipalities. This outlook might lead to an increasing flow of federal aid to the states with few strings attached. We are speaking of an inclination that is only partly realized, not of a fact accomplished. Meanwhile (as this chapter will argue), reasons of another sort exist for strengthening the role of the states without lessening the flow of support to the lower units of government.

In the fiscal year that ended in 1969 the national government paid directly to local governments an estimated total of slightly above two billion dollars. Approximately 72 of 429 national grant authorizations that existed in the middle of 1970 provided for payment directly to local governments. What is important in the present context, however, is not so much the great (and growing) importance of federal grants to the localities as the continued predominance of the states as the major recipients of aid in the national grant-in-aid system.[1]

THE MINIMUM ROLE OF THE STATES

The role of the state governments is indispensable. Their legislation is needed increasingly. It is true that today as well as historically the states generally contribute to the support of local government. But their plenitude of legislative powers and their laws on many matters are likely to be even more important. Various controls, hitherto conducted locally, must be lifted to the state level, although some can be undertaken by the counties. The upward shift (as in zoning and subdivision controls) is especially needful so long as the core cities are ringed about by well-to-do suburban munici-

1. Advisory Commission on Intergovernmental Relations, *State Involvement in Federal-Local Grant Programs: A Case Study of the "Buying-in" Approach* (Washington, D.C.: U.S. Government Printing Office, 1970), p. 2, drawing on the study by Carl W. Stenberg.

palities. A sign of the problem is the fact that the core cities have ceased to be able to grow by annexation in many parts of the country. The recapture, extension, and vigorous use of certain state and county powers are imperative needs.

Reflective of a potentially more active role for the states is the spread of state involvement in programs of urban and other local development, as shown by the pioneering of a dozen states. The entrance of the states was betokened at the beginning of the seventies by the phrase "buying in," indicating an option that should be open to actively interested states. It signified an alternative to the "direct federalism" that had been growing in the national-local types of programs. The possibility was summarized in the 1970 annual report of the Advisory Commission on Intergovernmental Relations. "The Commission," it said, "has been on record since 1964 in favor of a compromise: the states should regain administrative and financial control of local programs through buying in—putting up a substantial portion of the non-federal share of program costs." This comment was based on a survey of a dozen federally aided urban programs: low-rent public housing, urban renewal, urban planning assistance, model cities, airport development, urban mass transit, community action, waste treatment facilities, air pollution control, juvenile delinquency prevention and control, solid waste disposal, and aid for educationally deprived children. Most of the states replying had said that they were making some kind of a contribution, but more than half of the total amount reported was given in New York State alone. For the states generally it was noted that their technical assistance to localities was much better than their financial aid.

Looking to the future it is in point to mention New York's participation in the national program for federal aid in airport construction. A survey by Carl W. Stenberg found that it had notably improved cost-sharing arrangements, had widened the scope for local programs, and had lessened the costs for localities. At the same time the study indicated that "buying-in" had not increased the amount of state supervision of local projects. Significantly, state action had shortened the time for the processing of projects.

The need is growing for a more consistent policy in the respective roles of the states and municipalities. An advisory report in 1969 noted that some of the clashes between cities and states reflect an uncertainty over which layer of government may receive the major share of national funds and how responsibility is to be allocated. It was noted that in the past "most of the real initiatives have been taken by the larger cities leaving state government and most smaller cities with lesser pickings."[2] In housing programs (except for special groups like the elderly) most states were found to have played a minor role. Meanwhile, the smaller cities, lacking in skills and sometimes in leadership, had often failed to take profit by grant-in-aid programs. The advisory report suggested that the state governments could be useful in the housing field by providing "direction, technical assistance, and supplementary funding" in aid of the smaller cities. Nevertheless, even in the late sixties, it was found that "only a handful of states had even begun to develop state housing goals and even fewer had begun to implement them."

What has been said does not deny that many states have improved their means of contact with the national government. Even before the end of the sixties, at least half had established offices in the national capital. Governors generally had assistants or coordinators for national-state relations. Many had already established full-time planning staffs. The spirit was shown in a Connecticut law in 1967 that created a state department of community affairs. It declared that "the municipalities of this state do not have adequate resources to deal effectively with these physical, economic, and human resource problems and that financial and techni-

2. National Commission on Urban Problems, Research Report No. 17, "New Approaches to Housing Code Administration," 1969, pp. 195–96.

cal assistance by the state, in addition to that now authorized, and the granting of new powers and authority to municipalities are essential to enable the municipalities to plan,
develop, and conduct physical, economic, and human resource programs for effective community development."

The need to shift certain powers to the state level, or at
least to the counties under state laws, is entirely compatible
with the practice of home rule. Phases of home rule exist
under the constitutions of a majority of the states, having
spread since its beginnings in the seventies of the last century. Municipal governments of significant size, and counties
increasingly in many parts of the country, should be lib-
erated under charters of their own making to adventure in
many things. Their needs are variable and even more so is
the pacing that changes with leadership. This leeway is not
inconsistent with the requirements of the cities for financial
help from the taxable resources of the still larger units of
government. Nevertheless it is true, as Joseph D. McGoldrick
remarked in the early thirties, that among the handicaps of
the home rule movement "is the absence of a mechanism for
the handling of problems in which there is both state and local
interest."[3] The solution lies in services at the state level,
supplemented in many areas by the national government. At
the same time it is increasingly apparent that controls of certain kinds must be exercised at a level above the municipalities. This step is necessary, if only to rescue the cities from
their cramping encirclement by smaller and richer municipalities.

THE UPWARD TRANSFER OF CERTAIN CONTROLS

A major need is the upward transfer and the enlargement of
certain controls that for long have been exercised locally.

3. Joseph D. McGoldrick, *Law and Practice of Municipal Home Rule 1916-
1930* (New York: Columbia University Press, 1933), p. 317; supplementing the
classic treatment by Howard Lee McBain, *The Law and the Practice of Municipal Home Rule* (New York: Columbia University Press, 1916).

Zoning, for example, for many decades has been a captive of the smaller local governments. In the late sixties zoning ordinances existed in nearly seven thousand municipal units and in about two thousand townships. The fringe places were fearful about the expansion of the core cities; consolidations were opposed in part because of the fear of changes in zoning and related matters. This fact is not a reason in itself for enlarging the areas of general local government. It is a reason for looking carefully at the legal factors that have conspired to keep poor families within the core cities. This problem illustrates the need for shifting upward the exercise of zoning and related controls. Much power can properly be vested in the counties. It is at the state level, however, that there is the necessary amplitude of legal powers. The revision of the state laws that govern such things as zoning need not wait upon the financial and other involvements of the states in local affairs.

In these matters the state legislative role is indispensable. It is not an argument against this needed action, nor an argument against the nation's concern about city problems, to note that as late as 1970 (replying to a questionnaire) about two-thirds of the spokesmen for cities of 100,000 and over said that the national government had been more helpful than the state governments. National participation at all levels is indeed a natural feature of changing federalism in an urbanizing society. But this fact is consistent with the use by the states of their reserve powers in coping with the locally conflicting elements that are often concealed by the word "metropolitan."

An important aspect of the problem was shown in a comment of the President's Committee on Urban Housing. "It makes little sense," said the report, "for federally subsidized housing to be concentrated in and around central cities' slums where social and environmental disadvantages can negate the uplifting qualities of decent housing."[4]

4. *A Decent Home,* Report of the President's Committee on Urban Housing (Washington, D.C.: U.S. Government Printing Office, 1968), p. 13.

The salient feature of zoning has been the division of a jurisdictional level into zones or districts with uniform regulations for each but with differing requirements for each type of zone. The differentiating restrictions appeared mainly in such things as specified limits (usually minimum) on lot size and on the size, height, and placing of structures. The control also involved stipulations about the uses to which the land or structures might be put. Most of the numerous jurisdictions possessed of zoning powers have been small in area and population. The standards for residential building under these governments often forbade practices that were permitted by the "model" building codes. It was noted in the late sixties that less than one-sixth of all cities and towns of five thousand population and over had building codes which had been updated to conform with the advisory "model" code requirements formulated by the Commerce Department in the national government. In the years since mid-century only about a quarter of the recently adopted or revised local codes included 90 per cent or more of the updating changes embodied in the "model." But deeper and more lasting reasons than such tardiness call for the upward shift of control over zoning and related matters.

The delocalizing of zoning and related controls are among the country's vital needs. Such a movement, whether to the county level under state law or wholly to state administrative auspices, is desirable, if only to fortify urban government. It is instructive, however, to remember zoning's history and its useful role in the past. As a control it was inconceivable before some early experiments in California and Massachusetts. Slowly after about 1915 it gained acceptance in the country. Its legality remained doubtful until a Supreme Court decision in 1926.[5] Basically it was found that different districts in a community vary sufficiently from each other to justify the imposing of different regulations. The decision

---

5. *Village of Euclid* v. *Ambler Realty Co.,* 272 U.S. 365 (1926). Already the court had upheld a statute that limited the height of buildings. *Welch* v. *Swasey,* 214 U.S. 91 (1909).

noted that building zone laws were of modern origin. "Until recent years," it said, "urban life was comparatively simple; but with the great increase and concentration of population, problems have developed, and constantly are developing, which require, and will continue to require, additional restrictions in respect of the use and occupation of private lands in urban communities."

The court's ruling confirmed the view that the public interest in land use, as voiced in a zoning ordinance, prevailed over private property rights. Thereafter the legality of zoning was not doubted; the issues turned on questions about its application in particular circumstances. Complaints continued to be heard about the vagueness of zoning ordinances and the like on many points. Moreover, the ordinances themselves were sometimes brushed aside in various situations, usually for reasons of favoritism. Meanwhile, as has been noted, the national government was seeking to play an advisory role. Its revised model included the idea that the purposes in view "shall be made in accordance with a comprehensive plan." The scheme as a whole assumed that the restrictions would be uniform within each zone and that these would be mapped in accordance with a plan.

Meanwhile, growth within the "metropolitan" areas had brought a threefold reflex. One effect had been to give zoning powers to local governmental subdivisions other than cities, notably to townships and to counties. The result was what has been called a "mosaic of zoning ordinances in metropolitan areas." The vogue of zoning seemed to assure its spread beyond the urbanized areas. Only in some cases were certain types of zoning action subject to review by a governmental agency with more than a locally territorial coverage.

After World War II support weakened for the localized regulations associated with zoning. Previously both zoning and subdivision controls had been widely seen as successful and adequate for safeguarding growth and development. But spreading criticism came to be heard, partly from the charge that crucial decisions about land use were in the hands of too many uncoordinated units of government. It was said of land use controls that the unhappy result, if not the motive, was making it additionally difficult for low-income minority families to live in many urban places. Such complaints had many angles. It was charged that excessive zoning restrictions and subdivisional standards were blocking the building of low- and moderate-cost housing. In some places zoning for large lots was a method of preventing non-white families from living in suburban communities. It was said that zoning had failed as a vehicle for comprehensive planning. Meanwhile, apart from rumors of favoritism, these controls were not preventing wasteful urban sprawl in many places. Among the other complaints was the argument that antiquated and rigid zoning ordinances in many localities were preventing the use of novelties of design, such as cluster subdivisions, that would bring advanced standards for families that previously could not afford them.

The emerging needs point to basic state laws with certain controls no lower than the county level except in the case of large cities. These controls should touch several matters. They should prohibit the exercise of land use regulation by local units other than municipalities over a specified minimum population. They should require the referral of municipal land use regulations to the county level at least, allowing it a veto over local actions. Meanwhile, each state, in addition to setting basic requirements with such devolution to the counties as is deemed suitable, should provide financial support for a program of local planning assistance. Thus the system will rest fundamentally on the state's law and its administrative apparatus with less devolution of zoning and related powers to a host of small municipalities than prevailed in earlier decades.

The needed transition, whose beginnings can be seen already, was forecast by Paul Douglas as chairman of the national commission on urban problems.[6] Fragmented land use controls, he said in summary, had contributed to an unwholesome competition between the parts of urbanized zones and had prevented planners from giving attention to needs that should help to bind communities together. The zoning power, bestowed separately upon a host of governmental units, had become a method by which these governments, and particularly the small ones, had sought to shape things defensively within their boundaries. Chairman Douglas himself, in prefacing a companion report, noted that the "coming decisions are not trivial." He added: "They have important effects on broad social and economic questions, such as racial and economic segregation, access to job opportunities, and the role of local taxation."

THE REAPPORTIONMENT OF STATE LEGISLATURES

The upward shift of crucial powers that has been indicated should not and need not wait upon the probably slow and uneven effect of state legislative reapportionment. The Supreme Court's landmark decision in 1962 on malapportionment in legislative bodies started a movement with profound, if mixed and still unresolved, consequences.[7] It announced the basic doctrine that is popularly summarized as "one-man, one-vote." Within a year the court applied the rule to the election of statewide officers. Soon it held that the members of both houses in a two-chambered legislature must be chosen in districts of roughly equal population. Previously in eight states the malapportionment had been such that a majority of the state senate could be elected by one-fifth of the voting population.[8] Among the lower houses

6. National Commission on Urban Problems, Research Report No. 18, "Fragmentation in Land-Use Planning and Control," 1969, p. 1.
7. *Baker* v. *Carr,* 369 U.S. 186 (1962), correcting the effect of *Colegrove* v. *Green,* 328 U.S. 549 (1946).
8. Robert B. McKay, *Reapportionment: The Law and Politics of Equal Representation* (New York: Twentieth Century Fund, 1965).

there had been only ten where a popular vote of more than 40 per cent was needed to win control. In correcting such situations the Supreme Court went on to apply the rule of "one-man, one-vote" to local legislative bodies. The recoil against the foregoing decisions soon lost most of its force. For a time there had been agitation for a constitutional amendment that would allow one of the legislative chambers to be chosen without regard to the rule of "one-man, one-vote."

Only the unique position of the United States Senate under the constitution exempts it from the general principle of equal numerical representation. Historically the Senate's structure, with each state represented by two senators regardless of population, was the outcome of a famous compromise in the constitutional convention of 1787. But on occasion during later decades the equal representation of states in the Senate has been an important and constructive factor in the country's politics. It widened the foothold for agrarian protests in the late nineteenth century and afterward; it helped to give a national forum in which to speak against the country's rampant industrialism. Later in the new century the nature of senatorial advocacy shifted but grew in importance. Members of the Senate became outstanding as spokesmen for urban problems. This outcome is heightened by the frequently crucial role of the city vote in close statewide elections. Roscoe Martin (incidentally to his trenchant portrayal of urban needs and policies in concert with the national government) had reason for saying: "The most democratic legislative body in the country is the United States Senate, whose members represent the largest and most highly generalized constituencies."[9]

It is important to add that the leverage is not confined to the United States senators with help from the unique structure of the upper chamber of Congress. The state governors

9. Roscoe C. Martin, *The Cities and the Federal Government* (New York: Atherton Press, 1965), p. 192.

are chosen by a statewide vote. This fact encourages many
of them, with the state administrative apparatus at hand and
with the influence their office affords them, to give attention
to the problems of the cities.

Admittedly, reapportionment in legislative bodies does
not automatically help the core cities with their relatively
stable or declining populations. The immediate beneficiaries
of legislative reapportionment are likely to be the suburban
areas, organized as moderately sized cities or as villages. Reapportionment, though potentially significant, has immediate
and important effects only in special circumstances. Indeed
the early effect was often a strengthening, or at least the preservation on a new base, of many conservative forces in state
politics. The mayor of a large eastern city was heard to say:
"Reapportionment has suburbanized the legislature and the
suburbanites are as hostile to the city as the farmers ever
were." Moreover, although the trend of reapportionment
has been toward the equality of population among legislative districts, the court decisions through the sixties did not
interfere with gerrymandering.

It will be helpful in the future to give the duty of reapportionment after each census to some agency other than
the state legislature itself. A survey in the fifties showed that
in the eleven states employing this method the legislative
seats had been reapportioned within the past decade. In contrast no reapportionment had been made within ten years in
twenty-two of the thirty-four states where the responsibility
rested directly with the state legislature. In thirteen cases
there had been no reapportionment in twenty years.

Reapportionment is, however, only one of the influences at
work. The factors are many and mixed. A new tone has appeared in many legislatures. The average age is dropping.
Even where the dominant theories are conservative, the outlook is more positive. The shift of attention includes a
mounting concern about problems in the core cities. By the
end of the sixties about half of the states, including nearly

all of the industrialized ones, had created administrative departments for urban affairs. In the offing was the probability not only that controls like zoning would be lifted to the county or state level, but also that many hemmed-in urban areas would be widened and reconstituted or at least that leeway would be opened to meet urgent housing needs. Such trends will improve the competence of state and local governments to deal with the ever more complex problems of an increasingly urban society.

TASKS AHEAD FOR STATE GOVERNMENTS

"It is difficult," said a former governor, "for one not directly involved to realize and appreciate the full range of activities, interests, and services of state governments."[10] Their scope is wide and will grow, even if welfare generally becomes a direct responsibility of the national government. Meanwhile, a pressing need is the enactment by states of the crucial controls of local government that have been described. The states, to be sure, differ in area, population, political sensitivity, and influence. This fact in itself forbids dealing with them as if they were all alike. James L. Sundquist says wisely that "federal-state relations have to be converted from a *legal* concept, in which the states collectively negotiate in the legislative and administrative processes for rights and powers that all of them then possess, to an *administrative* concept, in which the federal government exercises judgment as to how much reliance can be placed upon each state and reaches an individual understanding with that state governing federal-state administrative relationships."[11] This points to the need for flexibility and variation. It also assumes that the way is

10. Terry Sanford, *Storm Over the States* (New York: McGraw-Hill, 1967), p. vii.
11. James L. Sundquist with the collaboration of David W. Davis, *Making Federalism Work: A Study of Program Coordination at the Community Level* (Washington, D.C.: The Brookings Institution, 1969), p. 271.

open for the entrance of states that are ready to join in the
interlocked system for planning and administration. But a
need exists in all the states for basic legislation on matters
like zoning. As things stand and are likely to remain in the
federal system of the United States, only the state governments have the power to rationalize policy regarding important functions previously left to the local governments.

What has just been said is not an argument for the upward
shift of local activities generally. It is true that a presidential
commission on urban housing has warned that "the federal
government could assume full responsibilities for effectively
and rapidly developing the full volume of subsidized housing
needs to shelter millions of house-poor families." For this
purpose (continued the warning) the central government
could acquire sufficient land by condemnation, let contracts
to private builders for housing development, and own and
manage the completed projects. But the report cited did not
favor so drastic a step. It preferred to continue with an indirect approach. Nevertheless, it did add that, if the preferred
approach should fail in the coming years, "it could well become necessary to turn to the federal government as the
'houser of last resort' for the nation's low-income families."
Obviously the Commission hoped that this further modification of federalism would not be necessary.

The promise of help with a more comprehensive kind of
planning was foreshadowed by the national Demonstration
Cities act of 1966. At the time two-thirds of the nation's population lived in some 227 metropolitan areas. These areas,
though real in many respects, are essentially a census device.
Each, on the average, contains ninety governments; there are
over a thousand in the metropolitan area of Chicago and
more than five hundred in that of New York. In the face of
this situation the 1966 law sought to stimulate the interrela-
tions among various functions. It said that all applications
for grants or loans for certain physical development projects
within a standard metropolitan statistical area must be ac-

companied by the review and comment of an area-wide body that was authorized to do comprehensive planning for the metropolitan group of communities. This partnership, with aid also from alert state governments, is not less necessary because the "social and economic forces that are concentrating the poor in urban ghettoes are not of the cities' making." These words are quoted from the first volume of New York City's master plan called "Critical Issues," issued in 1969; it was written largely by William H. Whyte. A year later it was said in congressional hearings that the "problems of our stagnating rural communities, decaying central cities, and sprawling suburbs take different forms and cannot be treated with uniform, simple remedies."[12]

No region is free of poverty. Indeed, more than a fifth of the country's rural population are poor under the definition that is generally accepted, as against one-eighth of the urban population. In the mid-sixties it was estimated that 40 per cent were poor in the states of South Carolina, Georgia, Alabama, Florida, Mississippi, and Tennessee and 35 per cent in Arkansas, Oklahoma, Texas, Louisiana, and New Mexico. This fact highlights a universal challenge. Properly read, it emphasizes the responsibility of the states in connection with the municipal governments. It points to the need for basic state legislation (with selective devolution of responsibility on the counties) that will deal with certain crucial local problems, including zoning and related controls.

CONCLUSION

The Advisory Commission on Intergovernmental Relations reported in 1970 that public policy must not only accommodate itself to "the tremendous scale of organization and re-development." It must also lead. To leave things to chance and to the "competitive and contradicting policies of thou-

12. 91st Cong., 2d Session, Senate, Committee on Banking and Currency, July 1970, Vol. I, p. 26.

sands of local governments" is to invite economic and social confusion. Each state must have an urbanization policy. Many things must be lifted to the state level. The summons is heightened by what was said in the same report about the situation at the beginning of the seventies. "Suburban tax enclaves were sprouting, the white noose was tightening, and local government units were multiplying in the country's metropolitan areas. But most states stood aside."

The census of 1970 confirmed the knowledge that the bulk of the people of the United States are "urbanized," although the reckoning includes many who live in the suburban municipalities. The situation is a challenge to the states as well as the cities. It is universal in its implications. It calls for the type of state control that has been described broadly in this chapter. It also includes the stimulative and coordinating types of planning that are on the increase in the less urbanized groups of counties. We are called upon to look at the complex of local factors.

VI

———

The Federal Role in
Reshaping Local Governments

AN UNDERLYING PROBLEM OF FEDERALISM is the improvement
of general-purpose local governments. This need is a pervasive theme in the recasting of grants-in-aid. With the growing attention to urban problems it has become an outstanding issue. The rescue of the cities is stressed in devising ways
by which, along with novel forms of support, the central
government can encourage local planning under more comprehensive forms of structure. It is instructive to remember
that as late as 1932 the United States delegation at the International Congress of Cities was alone among the more than
forty countries represented in saying that no direct administrative relations existed between the cities and the national
government. Three decades later it could be said that there
is "no greater challenge in our age to the inventiveness of the
federal idea than the surging tide of urbanism."[1]

This does not mean that rural problems can be overlooked. The emphasis in federal aid has indeed shifted to
places of congestion. But the countryside contains much of
the poverty that exists in the United States. For many purposes, both in design and in the coordination of services,

1. Nelson A. Rockefeller, *The Future of Federalism* (Cambridge: Harvard
University Press, 1962), p. 47.

the area of single counties is too small. The opportunities that lie in this fact stand beside the succoring of metropolitan cities as main challenges in the development of federal relations.

A major problem is to escape from, or at least to lessen, the splintering of local government. Over twenty-one thousand special districts exist, most of them to perform a single service. During a five-year period in the sixties these special districts increased by almost one-fifth. Their use has been due in part to state constitutional limitations that are largely obsolete. It has been caused too by the timidity of existing local governments in tackling new problems. Some of the causes point to the need for shifting certain functions upward to larger governmental units. Broadly, the avoidance of special districts calls for the strengthening of the apparatus of general government with comprehensive local planning. In the mid-sixties the national government was administering forty programs of financial aid for urban development; more than a dozen departments and agencies were variously involved in some way. Half of the programs had been enacted since mid-century. In only four did the positively stated objectives for implementation locally include the adoption of comprehensive plans for urban development. A sizable proportion said that the projects should not be inconsistent with such local planning as might exist.

THE FRINGES THAT ARE SUBURBIA

It was noted in 1970 that the population of the country's suburban areas had doubled in only a score of years. Meanwhile, the white-black ratio in the suburbs had widened from 14 to 1 to 31 to 1. An example of the portent was Baltimore, nearly completely surrounded by relatively affluent suburbs and on the verge of having a black majority. Yet the United States Civil Rights Commission said at the beginning of the seventies that the withdrawal of national assistance would threaten most, if not all, of the suburban governments. They need money from the central tax pool to stay abreast of the need for schools, roads, sewers, and the like.

The shift from core cities to suburban communities began on a large scale after World War II. In the sixties upper- and middle-income whites were moving to the suburbs. Their reasons were many, including the avoidance of school integration, deteriorating services, rising costs, high taxes, and the increase of crime and delinquency. In this aftermath there was sorry truth in a comment made in 1969: "The poverty and social isolation of minority groups in central cities is the single most serious problem of the American city today."[2] The jobless rate for teen-aged residents in poor neighborhoods had risen from 19.9 to 24 per cent in the early seventies. For black youngsters it had reached 35.8 per cent.

Within two decades after World War II a profound change took place. Many metropolitan areas comprise "a set of lopsided communities." These consist of one or more "central" or "core" cities that are high in costs, surrounded by bedroom communities and industrial and commercial enclaves with tax bases that cannot be used effectively by the core areas. It was typical that local taxes in the central cities amounted on the average to 7.6 per cent of the personal income of the residents, whereas outside the central cities such taxes amounted to only 5.6 per cent of the income. It could be said that "particularly in the older metropolitan areas of the industrial Northeast and Midwest, we are confronted with a fiscal crisis not only in the major central city, but also in some of its smaller neighboring communities." As things were going, it was increasingly true that one sort of jurisdiction, usually the central city, had the acute problems while another sort of jurisdiction, usually the suburban municipalities, had the resources. In many places the political

2. Daniel P. Moynihan, "Toward a National Urban Policy," *The Public Interest,* No. 17 (Fall 1969), 7.

boundaries were making it impossible to apply area-wide resources to area-wide problems.

As the sixties ended, while taxes in the large metropolitan areas were taking a higher percentage of income in the core cities than in the fringe of outside areas, the quality of governmental services in the latter places was improving in contrast with what was provided in the inner cities. The differences were noticeable in education, for which expenditures per pupil were higher in suburban communities. Yet people in suburban areas, avoiding much, are tempted to believe that they are escaping from basic problems like air pollution. Enlightened self-interest, if no more, will teach how universal are these worsening hazards.

The gaps that must be bridged were illustrated by the situation in the state of New York in 1970. A study at the time showed that the per capita payments of state aid to the suburbs exceeded those to the half-dozen big cities by 2.6 to 1, with health payments 16.2 to 1 and highway payments 8.1 to 1. Commenting on these facts, the mayors of the six big cities declared in a joint statement: "Rather than receive a smaller share of the aid, the cities actually need a higher ratio of aid because they contain a much greater proportion of the needy and the disadvantaged citizens of our state."

THE CORE CITIES

The declining population of the big cities was confirmed by the 1970 census. (Meanwhile, the national population had grown by one-seventh during the decade.) Los Angeles and Houston were among the few exceptions. The sharpest drops were St. Louis, down 19 per cent, and Cleveland, down 15.6 per cent. Racial strife in the sixties may have speeded the movement. In the country as a whole the older, close-by suburbs may fare as badly as the parent cities. On the whole, however, the suburban municipalities are growing. Looking to the future, no one doubts that the cities are here to stay, in the United States as elsewhere in the world. It is this certainty that deepens the problem and complicates the financial arrangements it requires, not only immediately in a period of emergent crisis but also for the longer run in using the nation's tax yields. The main problem is the change in the social composition of the central cities. This aspect is more significant than the fact that the population is stationary and even declining.

Thus far in the United States the idea has lagged of building new cities of moderate size—places of one hundred thousands, say, where a person's workplace would be near to his home. The idea is alive, however. An informal gathering of congressmen and of national and state officials, sponsored by Urban America, has urged a program of national-state grants to help a system of local development corporations in assembling land and in constructing houses, utilities, and community buildings. Britain has built thirteen "new towns" since the early sixties, bringing to a score the number finished since World War II. It is unnecessary to speak of somewhat similar programs in other European countries. The ideal of sizable residential communities that are circled by open country and that have work places at hand with lessened need to travel is sound, although at mid-century it was said that the zest for moving to the "new towns" had lessened in England.

In many core cities of the United States the disadvantaged groups—blacks and Puerto Ricans—have increased disproportionately. Many factors interact. Opportunities for agricultural employment in the southern states have been declining. The nation as a whole, with the aid of machinery, is producing abundance from the land with barely 6 per cent of the country's workers engaged in agriculture. In addition, the movement of needy families northward is due in part to different levels of relief payments in the various states. This fact in itself is an argument for a national welfare system. But the incidence of poverty is not confined to the rural

South, for the urban side of it is acute. In New York City the relief rolls at the beginning of the seventies numbered more than a million persons, about 15 per cent of the population. From the standpoint of the country's politics conditions in the core cities will be highly significant in the coming decades. A report of the Advisory Commission on Intergovernmental Relations in the late sixties said with pardonable overemphasis: "the manner of meeting these challenges will largely determine the fate of the American political system. . . ."

The double migration has turned the core of many northern cities into black ghettoes. Politically, by 1970 it had helped to bring Negro mayors to some of the big cities and raise the number of black congressmen to twelve. Four big cities had Negro majorities in 1970 as against one a decade before. Seven other cities were more than 40 per cent black.

The important role of state aid to municipalities is not minimized by the growing case for national assistance. Historically state aid to localities antedated the main features of national grants-in-aid. Largely it was given for particular purposes, and this stimulative selectivity continues in many fields. But the over-all needs of large municipalities is quickening a movement for per capita state grants and for formulas of distribution that may help the cities even more. New York State in the seventies began to share one-fifth of its total receipts from the personal income tax with counties, cities, towns, and villages in the form of a general aid grant. Population was the main basis but the formula for distribution provided for increasing the grants to large cities. Apart from New York's special effort, it should be remembered that for the country as a whole about half of the money raised by state taxes goes to the local units. Doubtless in many states the share is not generous enough. But it may be assumed that many previously local functions will be shifted upward to the state level. Not all of these will be controls like zoning; some will be costly services. It is to the nation, not to the states generally, that the country must look in the future for the main additions in support of urban needs.

The concept of a "well-balanced city" was extolled as a guide in the Demonstration Cities and Metropolitan Development Act passed by Congress in 1966.[3] The act called on the national department in charge of aid for urban affairs to "consult with other Federal departments and agencies administering Federal grant-in-aid programs." It authorized a program of national assistance "in addition to that now authorized by the urban renewal program and other existing Federal grant-in-aid programs." These, it said, are essential in enabling cities to plan, develop, and conduct programs to improve their physical environment. They are needed to increase the "supply of adequate housing for low and moderate income people, and to provide educational and social services vital to health and welfare." At the same time, after mentioning the multiplicity and scope of governmental services that are needed in the rapidly growing areas, the law dealt with the need for the coordination of the applications for federal aid. It spoke of the desirability in many places of an "area-wide agency" that would be designated to perform metropolitan or regional planning.

The Programs for "Model Cities" and Community Action"

The collaborative program for Model Cities was an interesting venture in federal regulations. It was emblematic of the wish to test things out in particular places and without a narrow categorizing of the means to be used. The original idea was a demonstration in five or six cities. The number was increased to one hundred and fifty communitiés scat-

3. Public Law 89-754, 80 Stat. 1255, November 3, 1966.

tered through forty-five states, the District of Columbia, and the Virgin Islands. A salient feature was to confine the demonstration to 10 per cent of the population in each city. The scheme called for "widespread citizen participation." The mood of the times, reflected in other national laws that intentionally carried it further, brought an involvement of residents that often went beyond what was covered in the basic law and its amendments. Throughout, the official authorities of the area were to be in charge. Much of the success of the demonstration necessarily depended upon the soundness of the planning process in the community. Amid the conflicts that beset many communities—to which people are beginning to respond with an uneasy conscience but also through public policies—these plans are bearing fruit, although they are often more successful in revealing the clashes than in composing the issues.

The idea of community action was used by Congress in ways that left a wide leeway for the "solution of the critical problems existing in particular communities and neighborhoods." The law said (in speaking of the creation of a community action agency) that a community "may be a city, a county, multicity, or multicounty unit . . . which provides a suitable organizational base and possesses the commonality of interest needed for a comprehensive work and training program."[4]

The nationally stimulated program called Community Action was closely related to Model Cities in the urban projects of the sixties. Community Action was in part a training ground for the leaders of minority groups and for poor people generally. The price was the fact that a sizable proportion of the local civic and other leaders tended to lose confidence in the program. But a conclusion to this effect is hardly warranted with a thousand such action plans in existence throughout the United States. At least it could be said

4. Public Law 90-222, 81 Stat. 672, December 23, 1967.

that Community Action provided "an innovative agency which gave the poor their first social and political role."[5] It was also true that many of the programs "made faltering steps toward revising the method of delivering aid to the poor." In these circumstances one is not likely to find any universally accepted index by which to measure the experiment's relative success or failure.

Mingled Objectives: Home Ownership, Urban Renewal, Slum Clearance

Action through private facilities is prominent in housing and urban development. Some federal aid is mingled in it. Much of the legislation seeks to help private building and attendant financing, depending indirectly on the government's credit. This approach is not new. The basis for much of it was laid by the national housing act of 1949, which is likely to remain part of the foundation. The Housing and Urban Development Act of 1968 reaffirmed the goal stated in 1949: "a decent home and a suitable living environment for every American family."[6] The 1968 law went on to note that the failure to reach the goal, especially for many of "the nation's lower income families," was a matter of grave national concern. The law confessed that "the nation's housing is not increasing rapidly enough to meet the national housing goal. . . ." But the objective was repeated. Congress reaffirmed the national housing goal and spoke hopefully of achieving it within a decade by the reconstruction or rehabilitation of twenty-six million housing units, including six million for low- and moderate-income families. Important parts of the 1968 law looked to private housing to help programs that would not involve the state governments.

5. Sar A. Levitan, "The Community Action Program: A Strategy to Fight Poverty," *The Annals of the American Academy for Political and Social Science,* Vol. CCCLXXXV (September 1969), 75. See also his book, *The Great Society's Poor Law* (Baltimore: The Johns Hopkins Press, 1969).
6. Public Law 90-448, 82 Stat. 476, August 1, 1968.

Support for planning at local and state levels is a feature of the continued experimentation in national legislation for housing and urban development. The basic legislation of the fifties was amended at the end of the next decade in terms that make grants-in-aid available "to assist state and local governments in solving planning problems, including those resulting from the increasing concentration of population in metropolitan and other urban areas and the out-migration from and lack of coordinated development of resources and services in rural areas." The objectives included help in planning from the state level for cities with populations of less than fifty thousand. The law illustrated how far the evolving use of federal aid is departing from the requirement that national grants must be matched on a "fifty-fifty" basis. Under the new statute, though it is more conservative than many in retaining a degree of matching, the nation's share may reach two-thirds of the cost, except in special circumstances when it may go to three-quarters.

An objective of the law, moreover, is to encourage collaboration among local governments. The statute admits that government at the state and local levels is "handicapped in this task by the complexity and scope of governmental services required, the multiplicity of political jurisdictions and agencies, and the inadequacy of the operational and administrative arrangements available for cooperation among them." Into these words can be read an outline of tasks for decades to come. The law noted the gains that already were made possible by the provisions in various national programs for help in tackling certain area-wide problems. But more coordination was needed in conducting the national activities, along with additional cooperation by the state and local governments. This double purpose was to be helped by supplementary grants from the central government.

Authority for slum clearance goes back to the slum clearance title of the national housing act of 1949. The movement was expanded by the Model Cities act in 1966. The legislation sought to extend renewal programs to entire city neighborhoods, larger than conventional project areas, and to broaden them (notably under the 1968 law) by permitting unlimited acquisition of slum housing for purpose of rehabilitation.[7]

The varied outreach of the hopes that were embodied in the many parts of the 1968 law included a new section on home ownership for low-income families. It authorized the head of the national department of housing and urban development "to make, and to contract to make, periodic assistance payments on behalf of such home owners and cooperative members." The assistance would be given through payments to the persons holding the mortgages if they met certain requirements. This part of the omnibus law spoke of new technologies in the development of housing for lower-income families. It included assistance to non-profit sponsors. It sought to provide leeway for special mortgage insurance assistance. It spoke of the possibility of help through national home ownership foundations. Another part of the law dealt with the insurance operations already conducted by the Federal Housing Administration. The widely ranging provisions sought, among other objectives, to promote flexibility in the interest rates, to improve certain details in the terms of insured mortgages that cover multifamily projects, and to ease the mortgage conditions in connection with land development.

Another part of the law dealt with new communities. It announced the purpose of helping in the enlistment of private capital for the development of new communities. The head of the national housing department must certify to certain things before the state could make a guarantee. A limit of fifty million dollars was put upon the outstanding obligations that would be undertaken in connection with any

7. Daniel R. Mandelker, "Housing Codes, Building Demolition, and Just Compensation: A Rationale for the Exercise of Public Powers Over Slum Housing," *Michigan Law Review*, LXVII, No. 4 (February 1969), 637.

single community development. Thus the credit of the central government was made available. The law also said that supplementary grants may be made to state and local bodies in helping them to carry out various kinds of community assistance.

The law of 1968 further provided that "to facilitate more rapid renewal development of urban areas on an effective scale, and to encourage more efficient and flexible utilization of public and private development opportunities by local communities . . . the Secretary is authorized to make financial assistance available under this title to local public agencies for undertakings and activities which are carried out under a neighborhood development program approved by him. . . ." The law outlined the prerequisite conditions. They included the limitation that no application for help in planning and carrying out a neighborhood development program could be approved by the national department unless "the governing body of the locality has, by resolution or ordinance, approved the proposed program and the annual increment covered by the application" and unless the national department concluded "that there is the necessary capacity to carry out the undertakings and activities included under the program." The help might include loans and capital grants as well as grants-in-aid. In addition the national department, apart from interim assistance for blighted areas, was empowered to make supplementary grants where the interest rates were high on loans from other sources than the central government.

The multiplying of programs had risks as well as promise in the decades after mid-century. It was said in the seventies, for example, that as many as fifty different national schemes were in operation to overcome housing deficiencies. They included the construction of low-cost housing, long-term financing at less than market rates, rent supplements, and rehabilitation. A nationally sponsored effort to apply industrial techniques to home building was already in sight. In the program for the Model Cities a new emphasis was being given to the social aspects of community life. These included child day-care centers, legal aid centers, health clinics, playgrounds and swimming pools, as well as the improvement of the standard amenities that are illustrated in schools and police.

The pace of urban reconstruction seemed slow. It required eleven years on the average to clear a tract of land under the urban renewal program. Yet experts were saying that it would take the building of one dwelling unit every twenty-seven seconds to supply the housing that the country would need in the year 2000. Meanwhile, the relocation of displaced persons would require both the acquisition of land beyond the normal city limits and an adequate transportation system.

Building on the laws and programs that have been mentioned, a congressional statute in 1969 for housing and urban development dealt with matters that ranged among things as diverse as mobile houses and nursing homes.[8] Much of it rested upon various uses of national grants-in-aid. It spoke of "assistance to city demonstration agencies." Like many current provisions for federal aid, it did not overlook the need for training of personnel in furthering the objectives of the law. In support of the combined aims of the law it declared: "The Congress finds that the rapid expansion of the Nation's urban areas and urban population has caused severe problems in urban and suburban development and created a national need to (1) provide special training in skills needed for economic and efficient community development, and (2) support research in new or improved methods of dealing with community development problems." The project rested mainly on matching grants, but no more than 10 per cent of the total was to be available to any one state.

Important and even crucial in coping with the movement

8. Public Law 91-152, 83 Stat. 379, December 24, 1969.

of comfortably-off people from the core cities is the willingness of Congress to set standards of access for public housing in the fringe cities. At the beginning of the seventies an effort was starting to expand the authority of the central cities in certain regards. The head of the Department of Housing and Urban Development told a congressional committee that such a provision was "a necessary first step in ending the ominous trend toward stratification of our society by race and by income." He spoke of the need to overcome the resistance against building low-income units outside the central cities. Already it had been shown by a presidential commission that the predominantly white suburbs around the core cities often use their zoning ordinances, building codes, and other legal measures to block nationally aided housing for poor people. The emerging questions were not merely the willingness of Congress to act within the limits of its power but the scope of its leverage in a cooperative plan. It was shown early in the use of national grants-in-aid that its persuasiveness is limited in many situations. In the face of attitudes that abound in suburban municipalities, a major question is the possibility of state action that will find a substitute policy for lending the force of law in support of collaborative programs.

State Involvement and the Meshing
of Issues and Policies

Stress properly falls upon the roles of the national government and the cities themselves in the tasks of urban redevelopment and housing in the country as a whole. This fact, however, does not belittle the activities of many of the state governments. All of the states are involved in one sense: their powers are needed. Nearly half of the national programs require some state supervision or other activity. Many of the states are active in an additional sense. As early as 1962, for example, fourteen state governments were providing direct financial aid to localities for the construction of housing to be rented or sold. Loans were available to assist municipalities in meeting the local share of nationally aided renewal projects.

Moreover, insurance under national laws is likely to involve the states. Thus the provisions of the National Flood Insurance Act of 1968, though citing the need for national support, said that there would be no such help "unless an appropriate public body shall have adopted permanent land use and control measures (with effective enforcement provisions) which the Secretary finds are consistent with the comprehensive criteria for land management and use" as set forth in the law.[9]

Another congressional enactment called the Urban Property Protection and Reinsurance Act of 1968, after declaring that "the vitality of many American cities is being threatened by the deterioration of their inner city areas," says that "responsible owners of well-maintained residential, business, and other properties in many of these areas are unable to obtain adequate property insurance against fire, crime, and other perils." Accordingly the law seeks to provide a program to make available the necessary insurance. In this connection it calls for cooperating with the state agencies that regulate insurance, consulting with the National Association of Insurance Commissioners, and looking toward the creation of a national insurance development fund. The states share in this fusion of measures.

The issues of poverty mingle confusedly in the question of housing shortages. The complaint is sometimes voiced that "by attempting too much, each of our present housing programs produces too little. By attempting at one fell swoop to produce large numbers of new housing units for the poor, each program has managed to antagonize a substantial part of the population."[10] The complaint asserts that in seeking to

9. Public Law 90-448, 82 Stat. 476 at 572, constituting the "National Flood Insurance Act" and related measures.
10. Irving H. Welfeld, "Toward a New Federal Housing Policy," *The Public Interest,* XIX (Spring 1970), 43.

allay the grievances Congress has imposed restrictions that
limit the ability of such programs "either to produce very
many units or to help very many of the poor." Such critics
see a partial answer in a further separation of the support
that may be needed for new housing production generally
from the subsidies that will alleviate the housing problem of
poor families. Warnings of this sort should be noted. But in
answer it can at least be said that timidities in these fields
will not solve either the residue of poverty in the United
States or the seeming incapacity of the commercial market by
itself to produce the needed amount of decent housing in
any of the industrialized countries.

The national administration that took office in 1969
sought to make sure that the state governments had a part in
the Model Cities program and that the city halls had the final
say over the citizen boards. Broadly speaking, it sought to
stress the improvement of administration as a main objective
as against the earlier purpose to demonstrate in sample cities
how poor neighborhoods could be revived. One may recognize the seriousness of the problems of administration and
applaud efforts to resolve them while at the same time noting as probably accurate the forecast that "the serious problems of the cities will continue to exist in something like
their present form for another twenty years at least."[11]

COORDINATION IN RURAL AREAS

The need for constructive programs in rural areas is not
lessened by the gravity of the urban problems that have
been mentioned. In the late sixties it was said that 23 per
cent of all households outside the metropolitan districts
(which, as has been noted, include the well-to-do suburban
communities) were living in poverty. Later times hopefully
will celebrate as one of the glories of western societies, not

11. Edward C. Banfield, *The Unheavenly City: The Nature and Future of
our Urban Crisis* (Boston: Little, Brown, 1970), p. 255.

least the United States, that they not only treated poverty as a remediable condition but also were prepared to expand the definition.

It is true that much of the emphasis has shifted cityward. Partly this altered accent is made possible by the national policy, continued since the early thirties, of providing a form of public support for the prices received by farmers for certain agricultural staples. Such price support, however, does not touch many pockets of rural poverty. It was from this standpoint that a section on rural housing was included in the congressional act of 1968. It was also with this in mind that the President's budget message in 1971 proposed that the outlay of about sixteen billion dollars of general and special revenue sharing with the states and localities should include one billion dollars for "rural community development."

A main solution has been found in the use of larger areas than single counties and in a planning process that properly avoids a take-over of detailed operating functions. Even the United States Department of Agriculture, long accustomed to stress collaborative work in counties, came to accept the idea of multi-county planning and coordination. By the end of the sixties more than a score of states had by law grouped their counties into regional planning districts. The national government helped the tendency by a presidential decree that forbade the national agencies to disregard the state-created districts.

Such planning and meshing of programs in the multi-county areas will not mean abandonment of the many separate programs that have arisen. In recent decades they have multiplied and extended beyond the activities that were stimulated by the United States Department of Agriculture through the extension service and through the committees for agricultural price support. Even when programs are as different as the work of the Soil Conservation Service and the Farmers Home Administration, a kind of rivalry has often appeared. This rivalry can be smoothed by coordination on a wider scale without damage to the separate undertakings. Meanwhile, the composite objectives of these and other national and state programs can be explored with an eye to common needs and possibilities. A prime advantage of the multi-county unit for planning and coordination is the fact that it makes possible the maintenance of a full-time, paid staff. In the face of this asset; the older systems in rural areas are fading. The multi-county unit can afford support for the help that is needed.

Multi-county machinery, in short, facilitates the merger of planning and promotion. It can link together the official and the non-official personnel who touch common problems. The operating details of most of the programs must be handled at levels nearer to the communities. The multi-county job lies in promotion, design, mobilization of research resources, coordination of projects, and expediting efforts. They draw on public and private springs of influence that include minority groups. In this spirit the President's National Advisory Commission on Rural Poverty recommended the creation of multi-county development districts throughout the non-metropolitan areas of the country.

CONCLUSION

In one part of the Agricultural Act of 1970 Congress committed itself "to a sound balance between rural and urban America." The law said that this balance is essential to peace, prosperity, and welfare, and that, to achieve it, "The highest priority must be given to the revitalization and development of rural areas."[12] Race has rural as well as urban dimensions. Upwards of 40 per cent of the country's black population lives in the countryside. It is well said that, after the revolution that lay in "the rise of an urban way of life,"

12. Public Law 91-524, 84 Stat. 1358 at 1383, November 30, 1970, in Title IX on "rural development."

a second revolution was its diffusion over the countryside.[13] For the long pull, beyond the point where the curtain falls upon our foresight about things to come, the patterns of local government in both cities and rural areas may change, although the principle of elective self-government will not disappear in countries like the United States. It has been the task of this chapter to show the nature of the going programs and to suggest some of the foreseeable adjustments.

13. York Willbern, *The Withering Away of the City* (Bloomington: Indiana University Press, 1964), p. 10.

VII

Interstate and Regional Linkages

THIS CHAPTER surveys the horizontal relationships that arise
among the parts of a federal system. At least five kinds of relationships exist. The first is implicit in uniformity con-
sciously sought in state laws and regulations. Much of this
results from the copying of statutes from place to place, led
often by pioneering states. Some of this process is intentionally structured through the movement for uniform legislation that has been going on since the nineties in the last century. Second is the role of lawsuits between states with the
availability of the Supreme Court as the arbiter and the
source of a body of rules that are vital in the operation of a
federal system. Third is the fabric of interstate compacts that
are made with congressional approval and often with the
administrative participation of the central government. The
formalized understandings are usually called compacts. In
addition is the much wider use, mostly between adjacent
states, of written arrangements called agreements or memoranda of understanding that are used without submission to
Congress. Fourth are the regional bodies like river basin
authorities. Fifth and finally among these relations are the
associations, sometimes composed wholly of state officials,
sometimes mixing national and local officials, and sometimes
bringing together public and private persons. The axis in the

foregoing five types of relationship is horizontal: from state to state. Nevertheless, as has been noted, the vertical factor of national participation is present in various ways: as the source of a statutory model for imitation; in the role of the Supreme Court; in the approval of compacts; in encouraging and participating in regional structures; and as partners in many of the associations.

INFORMAL COPYING AND THE FORMAL DRAFTING OF MODELS

A crude but substantial progress toward uniformity comes through imitativeness of states in a federal system. There is in fact little original state legislation. When once a suggestion catches root and flourishes its seeds drift down the wind. Before the commissioners who were named in New York State in 1867 to revise its statutes had even completed their work they were pleased to observe that two important sections which were "entirely original with the commission and the product of considerable labor and research" had been incorporated with the change of only one word in the code of civil procedure of a Pacific coast state. In 1907, to draw an example from another field, the actuary of the state insurance department of Illinois worked out a modification of existing systems of valuation that under the name "Illinois standard" was widely adopted throughout the United States. Sometimes the imitation of sister states is too literal. The statutory provisions with regard to shipping in land-locked North Dakota (borrowed, it was said, from the New York laws) once contained the statement that "port, as used in this code, shall be construed to mean any place on a navigable river or lake." A related provision said that a vessel must be taken out of port by a pilot. Thus the verbiage contained enough salt water and tar to allay, even on the sun-baked prairie, any nostalgia that existed for masted waterfronts and the open sea.

Imitativeness: Its Role and Its Risks

The methods of achieving uniformity go far beyond the haphazard imitation suggested above. (1) The national government can exercise far-reaching leverage through its regulatory statutes and the ensuing regulations and orders. The fact that their mandatory scope is limited often makes it desirable that they be cultivated as models and that the over-all uniformity thus achieved be made a step toward interlocking administration. (2) In legislating for the District of Columbia, and even more through the investigatory and advisory agencies that Congress can create almost without limit, the national government offers many statutory patterns to the states and localities. (3) Yet more important is the fact that the expert services of the central government are the source of so-called determinations that are recognized by the states and given the force of law for intrastate affairs. (4) Associations of many kinds (as will be noted later in this chapter) can furnish models for statutes and regulations and also definitions and standards for use by all partners in the federal system. The common objective of the foregoing methods should be uniformity in crucial matters, flexible in nature, and with allowance for adequate administrative leeway. A wise strategy should aim at limiting while also sharpening the objectives of uniformity.

The unifying influence of a national regulatory law upon the states may begin even before its enactment. Speaking three years before the enactment of the food and drug act of 1907 and recalling that for nearly twenty years a pure food and drug bill had been introduced in every Congress, Dr. Harvey W. Wiley (in charge of the national research on the matter) observed: "(This) has appealed so strongly to the states that a great many of them in the last few years have adopted, word for word, the definitions which have occurred and still occur in that bill before the Congress of the United

States."[1] Once enacted, a national law profoundly influences the spread and improvement of state systems of control. It should be remembered, however, that with few exceptions national regulatory laws are based upon prior action in some of the states. Congress is often helped by being able to draw on state administrative experience and judicial interpretation.

In drawing upon state experience, Congress should avoid a premature crystallizing of weak averages. Over the years, however, a main difficulty has been not the cramping effects of emulating national legislation but rather the tendency of the congressional and state statutes to grow apart when the novelty of the national models passes. If unity is to survive it must provide for cohesion in growth. This result is furthered by identifying in the laws those matters in which standardization is imperative; this arrangement allows for variations that are permissible and even advantageous. The standardizing of certain points along with variations is helped by the administrative leeway that has been mentioned. It is assisted further by associations of administrators or by joint committees. Such arrangements call for the maturing of constitutional doctrines that uphold the right of legislative bodies to "adopt by reference" future changes that may be made in the standards. The readiness with which the enactments of neighboring states are copied shows the need for advice about the usefulness of certain variations.

The goal of a wise uniformity is helped by looking at the general problem in its local setting. Usually the most practical approach is found by weaving the thread of a common standard through the fabric of the laws, regulations, and administrative customs at all levels of government. It was noted at mid-century that in dairy products, fresh fruit, and vegetables the cooperation between the Food and Drug Ad-

1. *Report of the 27th Annual Meeting of the American Bar Association*, 1904, p. 639.

ministration and various state agencies had minimized conflict at the operating level despite the overlapping jurisdictions.

Few aspects of governmental practice are more suggestive from the standpoint of political theory than the problem of drawing the line between official and voluntary agencies of standardization, together with the ways and the extent to which the recommendations of the latter acquire force. Consultation is essential in the preparation of standards. Once they are made, however, they cannot rely upon merely voluntary acceptance. They need support even when their purpose goes no further than convenience. In the degree to which they are to be more than a consensus of self-interest, standards are additionally in need of compulsions which must for the most part be found in governmental action.

In maintaining uniformity there is need for expert centers of appeal to which questions on the application of standards can be referred. Even the most carefully formulated standard will quickly dissipate itself unless some provision is made to unify its interpretation. In addition there is a second and more important need for appellate bodies. Uniformity, as has been said, should provide the means of its own growth. Without this quality it cannot ask for universal adoption. A dynamic uniformity can best be achieved by making deliberate provision for progressive changes subject to the normalizing influence of some agency. There is a natural tendency to vest appellate jurisdiction of this sort in expert agencies within the national administration. The Bureau of Standards is such a body. In certain matters the Bureau of Mines has a similar role.

Standards involve an implicit evaluation that should relate so far as possible to the ultimate use of the article or process. Danger arises because it is easier often to base the prescription (as in assuring the quality of milk) on intermediate factors that are objective in themselves. Yet they may have only an indirect and sometimes mistaken relation to the human end that is served. This hazard makes it necessary constantly to reconsider the methods of appraisal and often to reshape or shift the standards in the light of their true purpose.

Institutional Aids to Uniformity in Certain Fields

Since 1892 a body called the Conference of Commissioners on Uniform State Laws has framed models of legislation on certain subjects for adoption by the states. Even some years later, however, it was noted that until a majority of the states joined the movement, "it was useless to recommend uniform laws except upon the simplest subjects and matters of whose utility there could be no doubt." As late as the third decade of the new century, although commissioners existed then in all the states, only about fifteen states were contributing financially in an official way.

Appropriately, the careful draftsmanship was done mostly by law school teachers as commissioners. Three to five years were often needed for the completion of a model law, which was then offered for adoption by the states. Proposals in controversial fields of social reform had slight support and little success. The models likely to secure wide adoption were on topics that mutually interested lawyers and the business community without running into political issues. By mid-century the conference had offered about a hundred model measures, but only fifteen had been adopted by as many as twenty-five states. It was at this time, however, that a significant broadening came by combining a number of measures in the uniform commercial code. This model is serving a double purpose: uniformity plus clarification of the law that governs commercial transactions.

Meanwhile, the American Law Institute had been launched privately with foundation support. Its objective is not to offer model bills for legislative enactment as such. Rather it seeks through experts in certain fields of the law to rephrase and renovate the guiding principles that have emerged from the common law and statutory enactments. The founder of this group, William Draper Lewis, explained its purpose in 1923. The hope, he said, is "to make clearer, simpler, and better adapted to the needs of life, the common law, so that our system of administering and developing law may not break down under the weight of reported cases."[2] He emphasized that "the restatement is not a codification of law to be adopted by the state legislatures and thus given a rigidity which would prevent the law having that healthy growth which is essential."

Looking back on what has been said in the foregoing paragraphs about informal copying and the formal drafting of models, the illustrations have shown the variety of sources and also the limitations of uniformity. Diversity is a virtue of federalism, yet standardization on many matters is desirable. A key need lies with the state governments which are the source of so large a part of the law that governs day-to-day dealings and the conduct of private as well as public affairs. Copying from state to state offers an advantage in federal systems. It is usefully supplemented by more deliberate and formal ways for the drafting of models for general adoption. In addition and increasingly in many fields the national government is furnishing models for state acceptance. Often they are based upon the controls that the central government can exercise under the constitution. Oftener, however, they arise in the conduct of permissive services.

INTERSTATE LAWSUITS: A MEANS OF ADJUSTMENT

The conduct of federalism generally has profited by the example of the United States in entrusting its Supreme Court with original jurisdiction in "controversies between two or more states." By mid-century there had been more than one hundred and twenty cases of this sort. The importance of the court's availability is shown by the fact that in at least four

2. *Report of the 46th Annual Meeting of the American Bar Association*, 1923, p. 89.

instances there has been a show of armed force between the states. In some suits "a state of facts was presented which, if arising between independent nations, might well have been a cause of war."[3] But the author of this comment added: "Most of these cases began with hard feelings, and ended with placid and unvexed acceptance of the decision." The court's constitutional duty to decide interstate controversies and the availability of this prestigeful tribunal in disputes between states were from the start an asset in the workability of federalism. The constitution had improved upon the congressional handling of such disputes under the Articles of Confederation.

The availability of the Supreme Court and its equivalent in other federal systems in disputes between and among states does not lessen the importance of national legislation or of the administrative handling of questions under such laws. But sometimes there is no national statute and no power to enact one that could bear authoritatively upon the interstate dispute. The United States Supreme Court, in handling the suit between Kansas and Colorado about the former's claim to use water from eastward flowing streams whose source is in Colorado, said that in such cases the court is in effect weaving a fabric of common law for the adjustment of disputes between the states.[4]

Evolving Types of Issues for
Supreme Court Settlement
Boundary disputes between states were the type of interstate controversy that first came before the Supreme Court. Its jurisdiction here was clearly confirmed in 1838.[5] Such questions remained the chief source of interstate litigation. The court often named a referee (sometimes a surveyor) as its agent in marking the exact line in accord with the findings

3. Charles Warren, *The Supreme Court and Sovereign States* (Princeton, N.J.: Princeton University Press, 1924), p. 38.
4. *Kansas* v. *Colorado*, 185 U.S. 125 (1902).
5. *Rhode Island* v. *Massachusetts*, 12 Peters 657 (1838).

and decision. In 1970, for example, the Supreme Court closed a boundary dispute between Arkansas and Tennessee by declaring: "We affirm the Master's report."[6] But other interstate issues are growing in importance. The conflicting claims to water from interstate streams has already become the second main source of litigation among the states.

The Supreme Court's methods in handling suits about water rights between and among states were shown in its 1963 decision in the case brought by Arizona against California.[7] It was not the first nor is it likely to be the last of the interstate suits over the water of the Colorado River. The groundwork done by the special master (whom the court appointed) was basic to the disposition of the case. In the course of two years he listened to more than three hundred witnesses, developed a transcript of the hearings that ran to about twenty-five thousand pages, and embodied his findings and conclusions in a printed volume of more than four hundred pages, with a suggested decree for the court to issue. The Supreme Court itself listened to argument on two occasions, once for sixteen hours and once for six hours.

In disposing of the suit the Supreme Court modified the master's findings and conclusion in some respects. These changes were agreed to by Arizona, Nevada, and the national government. The Supreme Court took account of the fact that the situation as a whole already involved the operation of "a whole network of useful projects." It is worth adding, as an example of the flexibility that is often useful in these matters when the court has settled the main points, that the Supreme Court said: "Rather than adopt the master's decree with amendments or append our own decree to this opinion, we will allow the parties, or any of them . . . to submit before September 16, 1963, the form of decree to carry this opinion into effect, failing which the court will prepare and enter an appropriate decree at the next term of court."

6. *Arkansas* v. *Tennessee,* 397 U.S. 88 (1970).
7. *Arizona* v. *California et al.,* 373 U.S. 546 (1963).

The courts themselves, not least the Supreme Court, have confessed the limits of litigation. The court can establish boundary principles but seldom can it trace the exact line in all its details. That task and tasks more intricate and continuous remain to be handled by other means: by negotiation, perhaps, or by an interstate compact and the administration that follows. When New York sued New Jersey in an effort to check the discharge of sewage into the New York harbor, the Supreme Court agreed that the situation was a "grave problem" but added that "it was more likely to be solved wisely by cooperative study and by conference and mutual concession on the part of representatives of the states so vitally interested in it than by proceedings in any court."[8]

The essentially administrative adjustments that the court had in view need not take the form of a compact. Thus when North Dakota sued Minnesota in seeking to prevent the continued use of drainage ditches that were said to cause overflows on North Dakota land, the Supreme Court dismissed the plea without prejudice, saying that the somewhat conflicting opinions of the expert engineers should be turned over to "the consideration of the two states in a possible effort by either or both to remedy existing conditions in this basin."[9] It was indeed an engineering problem, not a legal question, but as a physical question it was not easily solved. In the decades that followed the difficulties have been eased but not wholly cured.

The Supreme Court takes a soundly pragmatic view of geography. Thus in a suit by New Jersey against New York, it upheld the right of New York City to divert water for the use of its people from the headquarters of the Delaware River, although that river flows *away* from the city and drains another watershed. Similarly the court upheld Boston's right to draw water from a tributary of the Connecticut River. But the court kept open the issue of possible fu-

8. *New York* v. *New Jersey,* 256 U.S. 296 (1921).
9. *North Dakota* v. *Minnesota,* 263 U.S. 365 (1923). ·

ture damage to interests along the lower Delaware River. During a later drought New York City's use of water from the Delaware River's upper tributaries was curtailed in pursuance of the ruling. This action showed the flexibility of the controls.

The Question of Enforcement

The enforcement of a ruling in a suit betwen states may raise delicate issues about an order that tells a state to do something. The matter is more easily handled when a duty is imposed upon administrative officers; the court can discipline them by holding them in contempt if its decree is not carried out. The situation is difficult when the legislature of a state must act. It is not easy to hold its members collectively in contempt. Moreover, where the issue is a debt, the Supreme Court may be reluctant to order the seizure of state property lest it cripple the state's governing powers. A long controversy in many stages was waged in the Supreme Court over West Virginia's duty to take over its share of Virginia's debt before West Virginia became a separate state at the time of the Civil War. The issues were finally settled in Virginia's favor when the Supreme Court declared flatly that the debt must be paid and that it would take whatever steps were required to effect this end.[10] The West Virginia legislature acted the next year, paying partly in cash and partly in bonds that Virginia had agreed to accept.[11]

The foregoing illustrations are enough to show the uses of interstate lawsuits under the jurisdiction of the Supreme Court. But the difficulties also suggest why other methods of adjustment often are preferable.

INTERSTATE COMPACTS AND AGREEMENTS

The mention of interstate compacts in the United States constitution appears in section 10 of the first article, which

10. *Virginia* v. *West Virginia*, 246 U.S. 565 (1918).
11. 1919 West Virginia Acts (Extra Session), Chapter 10.

declares that "no State shall enter into any treaty, alliance, or confederation," adding that "no State shall, without the consent of Congress . . . enter into any agreement or compact with another State, or with a foreign power." In form this language is a prohibition. In practice it has been an authorization for the making of compacts with congressional consent. Experience shows that the device fits two kinds of situations: "First, controversies between two or more states that abstractly may be fit subjects for litigation but which, because of the nature of the issues—the range, the intricacy, the technicality of the facts—make a court a very ill-adapted instrument for settlement; the second class comprises situations which are wholly beyond the process of adjudication."[12] Ordinarily a compact is made between two or more particular states, though sometimes it is more open.

Interstate reciprocity is on the borderline. It rests upon contingent laws in two or more states. Such legislation, though less perfect than a compact, is often more convenient. In reciprocal lawmaking each state is bound only if the other state does what is agreed upon. Reciprocity has been general in fields like professional licensing. Usually it is left to some administrative agency to decide whether the other state is complying with the arrangement. The Supreme Court seems to have left open the question whether the reciprocal arrangement should have congressional approval.

The Number and Variety of Compacts in the United States

By 1971 a total of a hundred and sixty-nine interstate compacts had been approved by the participating states and by Congress. A few others had been drafted but had failed of adoption in the state legislatures; a small number had been accepted at the state level but not by Congress. On occasion

12. Felix Frankfurter and James M. Landis, "The Compact Clause of the Constitution—A Study in Interstate Adjustments," *Yale Law Journal*, XXXIV, No. 7 (May 1925), 705.

there had been failure to complete the negotiation of the draft of a compact: even compacts that are nearly complete may be shelved in the light of new developments.

A salient point in the widening use of compacts is the fact that no continuing machinery was provided under the twenty-four compacts that were approved between 1783 and 1900.[13] In contrast, half of the seventy-seven compacts between the latter date and the mid-fifties provided for administrative arrangements of an enduring nature. This fact suggested the increasing use being made of the compacts for administrative purposes. The passing years give growing support to the forecast that "compact agencies may become a widely accepted and familiar governmental form in the United States."[14]

In some federal systems, especially those in Europe with its closely grouped but separate countries, the compact is useful internationally. The Swiss constitution has an authorization that is especially sweeping. The member states are allowed to make agreements, not only among themselves on legislative, administrative, or judicial matters, but also to make "treaties" with foreign governments in regard to the administration of public property and on border and police intercourse.

In nearly all countries, whether federal or unitary, various forms of contact and contract among the local governments are inevitable. Even where explicit permission to make agreements or compacts exists, as in the United States, the overwhelming majority of the contractual and like agreements among the member governments or their administrative departments (as will be noted) are made without reference to the "compact clause" and without the congressional approval that is required in the constitution. In the

13. Weldon V. Barton, *Interstate Compacts in the Political Process* (Chapel Hill, N.C.: The University of North Carolina Press, 1967). See also Council of State Governments, *Interstate Compacts 1783-1966: A Compilation* (Chicago, 1966).

14. Richard H. Leach and Redding S. Sugg, Jr., *The Administration of Interstate Compacts* (Baton Rouge: Louisiana State University Press, 1959), p. 229.

United States arrangements between and among administrative departments of different states—arrangements always present, extensive now, and likely to grow as functions multiply—are a major though little discussed feature of federalism. They are more informal than the important device of interstate compacts.

The Scope and Enforceability of Compacts

The different senses of the words "agreement or compact" in the constitution are not clear. The fuzziness of the language and resulting doubt as to its meaning have kept the way open for the arrangements among the states that have existed from the outset and that abound in a host of governmental fields without congressional approval. Nevertheless, Congress has played safe in the presence of the coupled words. Most interstate compacts use the terms "agreement" and "compact" jointly. The Supreme Court declared in an early case that "the terms compact and contract are synonymous."[15] But the kinship of contracts and compacts, as thus avowed by the Supreme Court, does not vitiate a multitude of interstate agreements with a contractual quality that exist outside the compact clause. The legal enforceability of these arrangements is another matter, as will be noted in later paragraphs.

A key question in the use of compacts, as seen by the Supreme Court, is whether "Congress, by some positive act in relation to such agreement, signified the consent of that body to its validity. . . ." The court has noted the flexibility of the mandate, saying: "The Constitution does not state when the consent of Congress shall be given, whether it shall precede or may follow the compact made, or whether it shall be express or may be implied." On the whole Congress has found it desirable to act on a completed document after such hearings as may be necessary. Little use has been made

15. *Green* v. *Biddle,* 21 U.S. 1 at 90 (1823).

of advance permission to the states at large to enter into compacts.

Underlying the necessity for congressional assent has been the wish to guard against the risk of intrigues among the member states and the possibility of foreign entanglements. The Supreme Court in 1893 (in the opinion already cited) commented upon the line between types of interstate understandings that require congressional approval and those that do not. "We can only reply," said the court, "by looking at the object of the constitutional provision and construing the terms 'agreement' and 'compact' by reference to it . . . it is evident that the prohibition is directed to the formation of any combination tending to the increase of political power in the States, which may encroach upon or interfere with the just supremacy of the United States." In federal systems where there is a lessening risk of sectional intrigue or military juntas the view that has been stated about the reasons for congressional assent would appear less compelling. This is acknowledged in the spread of agreements that are not submitted to Congress.

Some perplexities have attended the question of the ways in which the consent of Congress may be given. Such consent has sometimes been given in advance; sometimes the process has been a double one with permission for the states to negotiate and with later approval of the completed compact; oftener the assent is given in a congressional enactment that also contains the full text of the compact. It is customary to have this sort of congressional validation, but on occasion the approval may be implied. Thus, ninety years after a boundary compact had been made between Virginia and Tennessee, the Supreme Court held that it had been approved in fact by Congress in recognizing the agreed-upon boundary in connection with its approval of judicial and congressional districts and other legislative actions.

The enforceable obligations of a participating state were shown by the Supreme Court in a case that arose out of the compact made by eight states for pollution control in the Ohio River system.[16] West Virginia was as willing as any member of the group to go along, including the appropriation of funds to meet the administrative expenses of the joint commission that was formed under the compact. But the state auditor challenged the state's right to pay the money. This refusal was upheld by the state court that acted originally in the matter. The United States Supreme Court, however, decided unanimously that West Virginia must make its contribution.

*The National Government's
Administrative Involvement*
The national government's administrative involvement is a phase of the increasingly mixed nature of many of the issues that are dealt with in the interstate compacts. Before 1921 all proposed compacts were drafted before their submission to Congress except for a few to which that body had given its consent in advance. In the case of the original Colorado River compact (drafted in 1922) the state delegates requested that a national representative be designated to sit with them. The request was granted, and the pattern became general.

The growing share of the national government, not merely in the initial approval by Congress and often in later rulings by the federal courts but also administratively, is stressed by Frederick L. Zimmermann as a current feature: "An outstanding new use has been to effect vertical coordination of national, state and local levels to supplement its interstate horizontal coordination."[17] He mentioned the Delaware River Basin Compact of 1961, which declares that its purpose is "to create a regional agency by intergovernmental compact for the planning, conservation, utilization, develop-

16. *West Virginia ex rel. Dyer* v. *Sims,* 341 U.S. 22 (1951).
17. Frederick L. Zimmermann, "A Working Agreement," *National Civic Review,* LVIII, No. 5 (May 1969), 201–5.

ment, management, and control of the water and related natural resources of the Delaware River Basin. . . ." The congressional act of approval not only gave its consent but also added: "and joins."[18] A national representative sits as a participant with delegates from Delaware, Pennsylvania, New Jersey, and New York on a body with broad functions that include the power to borrow money on its own credit. The compact is increasingly an adjunct of national action. The horizontal and vertical axes combine in a way that suits the spirit of federalism in accord with the growing sense and practice of interdependence. The use of the Colorado River's flow, for example, comprehended the national government's construction at Boulder Canyon and elsewhere in addition to the interstate compact about the stream flow from the upper to the lower parts of the basin. But the interstate promise of a minimum flow, to be monitored by the Geological Survey at a midpoint, is not enough. In later years the implications for concerted action have been carried still further. They include collaboration among the states in the upper part of the basin.

Nevertheless, this stress upon the combining of axes does not deny the importance of many border issues that arise and are likely to increase in a federation of fifty member states. An example of the possibilities ahead for services along interstate boundaries is the compact between California and Nevada that creates the Tahoe Regional Planning Agency as a legal entity with the duty of drawing a plan with regulatory powers. The agency is financed by appropriations from the involved counties in the two states.[19] The Susquehanna River Basin Compact, launched by an interstate agreement in 1970, is still another example of an agency for comprehensive multiple-purpose planning.

Still another revealing example is the compact between New Hampshire and Vermont for school districts that lap the

18. Public Law 87-328, 75 Stat. 688, September 27, 1961.
19. Public Law 91-148, 83 Stat. 360, December 18, 1969.

two states. Each such school district, says the compact, is to be "a natural social and economic region with adequate financial resources and a number of pupils sufficient to permit the efficient use of school facilities."

In North America the need for collaboration along the international boundaries is less pressing than in Europe with its many contiguous countries. But the handling of pollution as well as the maintenance of the water level in the Great Lakes involves international action. The issues are not new; the Supreme Court intervened many years ago to check an undue lowering of the level by the diversion of water through the Chicago drainage canal into the Mississippi. Growing concern about emerging issues nevertheless found expression in the compact approved by Congress in 1968 that brought together the representatives of eight states and three Canadian provinces.[20] Two years later the United States and Canada agreed formally that they would coordinate still further the programs to control the pollution that is bringing "death" to the lakes. It was emblematic of the merging of national and interstate action, along with the long-standing relationship through the International Joint Commission, that the compact did not displace the Great Lakes Basin Committee in the United States that was set up under the congressionally enacted Water Resources Planning Act.[21]

Meanwhile, the compact device grows in importance. Even more rapid is the growth of administrative agreements between the central government and particular states and between states.

REGIONAL BODIES

Increasingly the interstate compact is a regional device in which the nation shares. But regions are of the soil, indige-

20. Public Law 90-419, 82 Stat. 414, July 24, 1968.
21. Public Law 89-80, 79 Stat. 244, July 22, 1965.

nous and durable. They are also human, with varying contours that people shape through their achievements, their needs, and their movements. This section will look at the machinery that is arising to cope with regional problems. In this system the states group themselves into regions "based on both geographical contiguity and their place in the specialized set of communication channels through which flow new ideas, information and policy cues."[22]

By the seventies more than five hundred regional councils existed in the country; six out of ten of them had been formed after 1966. Slightly under half were in non-metropolitan areas. On the average they received 60 per cent of their funds from federal grants for functional types of planning. Nearly all were merely advisory, although some played a more active role.

In the face of difficulties that already are visible and widely discussed, like pollution in its many phases, the familiar remedies are not enough, although they draw advantages from things like tax incentives, grants, or loans to industry. Part of the answer is perceived to lie in "strategically located federal river basin authorities."[23] The efforts in the seventies and beyond will project what was begun inconclusively in the second and third decades of the century.

Only the Tennessee Valley Authority emerged from the early experiences as a going organization. Its auspices were unique, its duties diverse. The functions are so varied in their cumulative growth that Roscoe Martin could say truly that "the TVA is in an important sense a regional department of natural resources."[24] Certain national electrical un-

---

22. Jack L. Walker, "The Diffusion of Innovations Among the American States," *American Political Science Review*, LXIII, No. 3 (September 1969), 898.

23. Marc J. Roberts, "River Basin Authorities: A National Solution to Water Pollution," *Harvard Law Review*, LXXXIII, No. 7 (May 1970), 1544.

24. Roscoe C. Martin (ed. and co-author), *TVA: The First Twenty Years* (University, Ala.: The University of Alabama Press in concert with the University of Tennessee Press, 1956), p. 271.

dertakings that arose subsequently are more special in the purposes and the range of their local cooperation. Meanwhile, the separate departments of the national government, busy on their distinctive tasks, entered into loose arrangements that seemed a retreat to some people who had hoped for general adoption of the TVA idea. A development in the early forties was the formation of the Missouri Basin Inter-Agency Committee that brought together four national departments and a regulatory commission in company with five state governors serving on a continuous and five more serving on an occasional basis. This consultative device covered one-sixth of the continental area of the United States within which over a hundred dams were building or projected.[25]

In the mid-sixties a major step toward a fuller concert was taken by the Water Resources Planning Act.[26] Its statement of policy speaks of the "rapidly expanding demands for water throughout the nation." The President had already said that by the beginning of the next century the country will need two and a half times more water than it was consuming in the sixties. The law declares it to be "the policy of the Congress to encourage the conservation, development, and utilization of water and related land resources of the United States on a comprehensive and coordinated basis by the Federal Government, States, localities, and private enterprise." The statute sets up a national Water Resources Council and opens the way for river basin commissions. The council is given the duty to lay down (with presidential approval) principles, standards, and procedures "for Federal participants in the preparation of comprehensive regional or river basin plans and for the formulation and evaluation of Federal water and related land resources projects," and to "formulate such recommendations as it deems desirable

25. Rufus Terral, *The Missouri Valley, Land of Drought, Flood, and Promise* (New Haven: Yale University Press, 1947).
26. Public Law 89-80, 79 Stat. 244, July 22, 1965.

in the national interest." Such recommendations, together
with the views of concerned agencies and officials, go to the
President for his review and for submission to Congress.

The law took account of the planning ideal that has been
emergent since the thirties. The Water Resources Council
was empowered to approve any program for comprehensive
water and related land resources planning that was submitted by a state, provided the proposed planning program
showed evidence of full and complete consultation with all
interested parties and agencies, and provided further that
the program gave assurance that it would be in conformity
with the "general development policy" of the state. No such
program could be disapproved by the council without giving
reasonable notice and an opportunity for a hearing. The
scheme as a whole was to be helped by national grants-in-aid.

The statute authorized the President to "declare the establishment of a river basin water and related land resources
commission upon request therefor by the Council, or request
addressed to the Council by a state within which all or part
of the basin or basins concerned are located." Each such regional body would serve as a principal agency for coordinating the planning in the area for the development of water
and related land resources. Each would be presided over by
a chairman named by the President (who must not be an
active officer of the national government), with the duty also
of coordinating the interests of the national departments that
had representatives on the regional body. In addition, each
state would have a member chosen in accordance with its
laws, supplemented by a representative of each interstate
agency that might exist. The duties of the commission were
essentially to study conditions in the basin and to submit to
the council for transmission to the President and to the governors and legislatures of the participant states "a comprehensive, coordinated, joint plan" for water and related land
resources development in the area.

Somewhat similar but uniquely regional was the program

begun in the mid-sixties for the eighteen million people who live in Appalachia, an area which, covering nearly four hundred counties that spread across eleven states, is considered to be underdeveloped economically. The President named an areal study commission of state and federal members. Its report and recommendations led to passage of the Appalachian Regional Development Act of 1965, which voiced congressional acceptance of the hopeful findings of the presidential study group. The law, said the preamble, "concludes that regionwide development is feasible, desirable, and urgently needed.[27] It proposed to concentrate public investments "where there is a significant potential for future growth, and where the expected return on public dollars will be the greatest." The law created an Appalachian Regional Commission with a national co-chairman and a member from each state involved. Though the stress was upon rehabilitation in terms of economic feasibility, the statute suggested a number of special programs: highways; demonstration health facilities; land stabilization, conservation, and erosion control; mining area restoration; and a water resources survey. Broadly speaking, the program sought to improve the profitability of private investment by raising the quality of the regional resources and the social overhead of the area.

Almost at the time of the passage of the Appalachia law a measure called the Public Works and Economic Development Act was enacted by Congress.[28] It noted that despite prosperity in the country as a whole "some of our regions, counties, and communities are suffering substantial and persistent unemployment and underemployment. . . ." It was the nation's duty in cooperation with the states, the statute went on, to help the areas and regions in improving "their public works and economic development" and in establishing "stable and diversified local economies and im-

27. Public Law 89-4, 79 Stat. 5, March 9, 1965.
28. Public Law 89-136, 79 Stat. 552, August 26, 1965, amended by Public Law 90-103, 81 Stat. 257, October 11, 1967.

proved local conditions, provided that such assistance is preceded by and consistent with sound, long-range economic planning." One of the law's main parts provided for economic development regions (to be established with state concurrence) in places of need and for regional commissions. The commissions were not operating bodies; rather they were viewed as agencies for planning and coordinating. An observer could well say that the experiment was worth watching "both as a new instrument of economic development and as a new institution in intergovernmental relationships."[29]

A discerning critic said of the original legislation for area redevelopment that it was probably mistaken in assuming that all "depressed communities can be saved."[30] The solution may lie in equipping unemployed with skills that are marketable elsewhere and with assistance in moving there.

ASSOCIATIONS AS LINKS IN FEDERAL SYSTEMS

Associations of many kinds bring together officials and others who have a concern in the same line of work. Nearly every field of administration has such a body. As early as the twenties no fewer than fifty were listed; they have grown into the hundreds and continue to multiply as old domains are subdivided and new subjects (planning, for example) are recognized as distinctive disciplines. Recent decades have seen the appearance of separate groups like the National Association of State Budget Officers, the National Association of Sanitarians, and the National Association of Housing and Redevelopment Officials. The influence of these associations is mainly informal and indirect, as in the sharing of ex-

29. Edward F. R. Hearle, "Regional Commissions: Approach to Economic Development," *Public Administration Review*, XXVIII (January-February 1968), 15–18.

30. Sar A. Levitan, *Federal Aid to Depressed Areas. An Evaluation of the Area Redevelopment Administration* (Baltimore: The Johns Hopkins Press, 1964), p. 251.

perience. In some cases, however, an association develops standards of a fairly precise nature (through definitions or tests or procedures, to illustrate) that are recognized in administering the law in question and may be avowed expressly in the law itself. The associations contribute importantly to administration. Their advantages, however, are offset in part by their narrowly functional nature. This weakens the possibilities of a more comprehensive administrative integration at each level of government and is attended often by the risk of defensive conservatism. It is true that multipurpose organizations have increased, including national associations, but mostly they speak for particular levels of government.

The role of associations was illustrated in the 1970 law on occupational safety and health.[31] It referred to "national consensus standards." It defined them as meaning any safety or health norm that (1) has been adopted and promulgated by a nationally recognized standards-producing organization under procedures whereby it can be determined by the Secretary that persons interested and affected by the standard have reached substantial agreement in its adoption, (2) was formulated in a manner which afforded an opportunity for diverse views to be considered and (3) has been designated as such a standard by the Secretary after consultation with appropriate Federal agencies.

Scientific formulas evolve slowly in the experience of professions like medicine and in industries like pharmaceutical manufacturing. They gather in compilations that it is convenient for both statute laws and administrative officials to recognize. By dint of many and repeated references in legislative enactments the document called the United States Pharmacopoeia and National Formulary has been given virtually governmental status. It is revised periodically by an expert group. The law recognizes the current edition as the standard of purity for drugs and foods.

31. Public Law 91-596, 84 Stat. 1590, December 29, 1970.

Growing reasons of public policy insist upon many fundamental standards. At present they are mostly national, presently many will be international. The needs of a mobile population make uniformity a necessity. Already state laws are taking account, for example, of tests that are conducted by the National Board of Medical Examiners. They are an alternative to the accrediting examination in the applicant's former state or in the state to which he is going. A similar flexibility is achieved in many states by laws that recognize standards set by professional associations like the National Board of Dental Examiners and the Council of State Boards of Engineering Examiners. Increasingly also the state laws that regulate admission to the professions are requiring that the training be in accredited schools. This may amount to delegating a responsibility to professional associations of a private nature. The risks in this situation are a warning against carrying to excess a sound tendency.

The Narrowly Functional Cast of Most Associations

The associational device often begins in a restless reaction of kindred administrators against what seem to them an undue diversity among the state laws. At the outset there may be ambitious talk about the possible role of an association in standardizing legislation. An organization is formed. The quest for uniformity soon meets serious obstacles. The statutes of many states are already complex; the legislators seem indifferent; frequently a real diversity exists among the conditions in the various parts of the country. So the early interest in a uniform law is likely to come to nothing. If the movement lives on and the association becomes vigorous, it grows increasingly interested in certain administrative problems that the different jurisdictions have in common. The discussion of uniformity changes in its approach and emphasis. It becomes more concerned about a few key points in the medley of statutes and with administrative procedures. The association acquires more internal cohesion.

The many public or preponderantly public types of administrative associations originate in response to shared concerns. Mostly these concerns grow out of the interest of public officers in administering a particular control or service. Often it involves the collaboration of private persons in a mixed group. In federal systems especially, the structure and activities of the associations are affected by the fact that the government operates constitutionally at different levels. Administrative associations of a composite nature are invaluable in harmonizing these operations.

Administrative associations are often beset by the problem of allowing interested outsiders to attend their meetings. Courtesies extended are likely to backfire. For example, complaints were heard among the utilities commissioners about entertainments that were hurting the association's standing. A somewhat similar complaint has been voiced by the National Association of Insurance Commissioners. In still another field it is understandable that the members of an association of state highway engineers have a vivid interest in the new types of graders and tar-sprayers shown at the conventions of the American Road Builders Association, but this would be a questionable reason for meeting at the same place and time.

Many associations draw lines that seek to discriminate among members, guests, and onlookers. The association of public employment services opened its ranks to persons who were concerned about the problems of unemployment but barred them to anyone who operates "an employment agency for profit." In still another domain the institute of steam boiler inspectors confined its membership to "boiler inspectors employed by the Federal, State, and cities, and Dominion governments and the insurance companies of the United States and Canada." Many associations draw even stricter lines. Thus the nationwide assembly of fire marshals declined to affiliate with the National Fire Protective Association, although the marshals were glad to cooperate with such groups as the American Institute of Architects, the National Safety Council, and the National Board of Fire Underwriters.

Obvious reasons exist for the inclusion of Canadian members in many associations. Problems are shared at many points along an extended common boundary. The mutuality has not been confined to water resources. In milk inspection, for example, this international interdependence is shown in the recognition of a milk-shed that includes the northeastern states but also extends into Canada. Already international associations of administrators exist in many fields, and some of them do help in harmonizing and also tightening many procedures and rules. Thus do they draw the threads of functional union across international boundaries.

Expenses are a burden for many associations. State auditors in some places have complicated the problem by raising objections. Vainly in a Kentucky court decision did a dissenting judge challenge the majority of his colleagues by asking "If (national) meetings benefit business executives and the companies they serve, why should not the state and its large municipalities avail themselves of like opportunities?"[32] The majority's stand in this case remains a warning against undue conservatism. In the national government the General Accounting Office has sometimes questioned the expenses incurred in attending association gatherings. A related issue is the cost of publishing the proceedings. Much can be said for the plea of the head of a state department of agriculture at a meeting of his association: "I am spending quite a sum of money to come here and I would like my Governor to know I have gotten some good out of the meeting and I do not know how better to tell him than to have a printed report." In many fields of work where interlocking administration bridges the governmental levels the national government is able to publish the record.

The hundreds of associations differ and are likely always to differ in their procedures and influence. As a linkage they

32. *Shanks* v. *Commonwealth,* 219 Kentucky 212, 292 S.W. 837 (1927).

are potentially important in many fields of administration. Their performance is likely to remain uneven. Too frequently, perhaps, their gatherings follow a traditional type of conduct: a few general meetings in some noisy hotel ballroom with the reading of formal papers of dubious quality, without much relation to each other and listened to almost without discussion, along with some tedious committee reports. In these circumstances the real benefits come from the informal and personal contacts among individuals with common interests. Such contacts will remain important always, but hopefully the organization's targets can be better defined and the formal discussions sharpened.

Interlevel Associations of Broader Scope
A variety of reasons will continue to bring together associations of relatively specialized individuals in particular fields of administration. In the past these associations have tended to be vital in proportion to the degree of professionalism and the permanency of tenure of their members. During recent decades, however, a significant effort has been made to create and to galvanize nationwide and regional organizations of a more omnibus sort.

The Conference of Governors has had varying success as an organization.[33] Following several inconclusive efforts to bring the governors together in a lasting organization, a permanent Governor's Conference was launched with high hopes at the end of the first decade of this century. Soon it was languishing, although it continued to meet; its part-time secretary seemed to despair of making it a vital organization. Some executives, to be sure, picked up clues about budget reforms and like issues and testified to the value of the meetings. Much of the interchange, however, seemed to be talk about when the governors would make their try for election to the Senate.

33. Glenn E. Brooks, *When Governors Convene* (Baltimore: The Johns Hopkins Press, 1961).

Various attempts were made to help the conference. There was talk of financing it by a semi-public grant and at least one foundation stood ready to help. Doubtless part of the difficulty, in addition to the country's size and the number of states, lay in the relatively short term of the elective executives. The handicaps include the division of the governorships between the major parties. The issue of segregation has been a divisive issue, although few governors have cared to discuss it directly.

The difficulties survive but have not proved fatal handicaps. The staffing of the conference has improved. President Johnson cleared some of his messages with the governors. President Nixon, speaking to the Governors' Conference in 1969, mentioned a New Federalism and said that "power, funds, and authority are channeled increasingly to those governments that are closest to the people." But as a new decade began it was said in the daily press that the conference proceedings were "dismal" and "the almost total irrelevance of annual governors conferences has caused a reaction among some state executives." Meanwhile, much of the organizational vitality lay in the regional associations of governors.

For both state and local governments, other centers developed from older beginnings. The Council of State Governments grew out of the former American Legislators Association. Its headquarters (after some initial foundation help) are supported by contributions from the state governments. In each state it is linked to a commission on interstate cooperation which usually combines legislative and administrative members. The council's primary aim is to present the state viewpoint regarding national measures. At mid-century and after it seemed to stand militantly on the "states' rights" side of public issues.

In municipal affairs the U.S. Conference of Mayors arose during the depression of the thirties as a spokesmen for the large cities, whose needs it continues to espouse before Congress. Meanwhile, it had begun to admit smaller cities if approved by the conference's governing council. By the sixties its members numbered nearly six hundred cities. Much more numerous is the National League of Cities with over thirteen thousand members, joined at the state level into leagues of municipalities. The counties have their spokesman in the National Association of Counties, with an institutional membership that rests on the country's three thousand counties but emphasizes the urban (larger) counties and their problems.

A quite different kind of organization is the Advisory Commission on Intergovernmental Relations, which was created by Congress in 1959.[34] Its balanced board of twenty-six members brings together representatives of governments at all levels. The commission has assembled a competent and well-trained staff. It provides a valuable source of studies and reports, but is not a leader in controversial issues. How, indeed, can that need be met apart from politics itself?

CONCLUSION

The challenge that has just been voiced rhetorically is indeed fundamental. But to recognize it is not to gainsay the usefulness of the groupings that form at the high level where policy touches administration. This chapter has surveyed five kinds of unifying factors. In different ways they draw functional threads across the territorial division of federalism, involving variously the agencies of all levels of government. Thus the pattern is triangular. A significant need in federal systems is to preserve the vitality of the federal partners while achieving coherence in the operations of the government. The spirit of function, though strong inherently and destined to be durable, is yielding to this necessity.

34. Public Law 86-380, 73 Stat. 703, September 24, 1959.

VIII

Administering Federalism:
A Summary and Forecast

AMONG A DOZEN FEDERAL SYSTEMS in the world today, the distinctive constitutional form of federalism is most durably demonstrated in the United States, oldest among them if the confederal beginnings of Switzerland are disregarded. The scheme in many forms retains the basic idea of dividing powers between a central government for the whole area and a number of constituent governments under a constitution that cannot be changed by the ordinary method of national legislation. But recent trends and emerging developments are bringing profound changes. In the federal system of the United States, to be sure, much would remain unique if only because of its size in numbers of people and in the spread and diversity of its area. It is misleading to minimize the importance of these and other special characteristics in comparing the United States with other federations; to do so is to obscure rather than enlighten the features they have in common. At the same time a growing together of administrative methods is evident among the federal systems that now exist in the non-communist countries with technologically advanced economies. It is timely to summarize the outstanding developments with some guesses about the future.

THE SUPREME COURT'S CHANGING EMPHASIS

Crucial in present-day federalism is the judicial power to invalidate laws as well as administrative orders that trespass upon constitutionally guaranteed rights. The United States Constitution as drafted by the convention in 1787 contained few such guarantees; it was assumed that protection enough existed in the fact that the central government (which at the time was seen as the chief source of danger) has only delegated powers. The doubts that were voiced during the process of ratification showed that this source of protection was not considered to be enough. Accordingly, in 1791, the United States pioneered in adding a "bill of rights" to its constitution. The newer federal systems have done well in adopting this safeguard. Its use in the United States is growing as a check on government at all levels—national, state, and local.

At the same time the courts are more and more chary about invalidating statutes of a regulatory nature if they are carefully drawn. This judicial tolerance also extends to state legislation on economic matters, provided that the action is not inconsistent with the national constitution or in conflict with a congressional enactment. Increasingly in the decades since the thirties the courts have allowed a wider scope for state and local action, both in regulating things and in the use of taxing powers, so long as this action does not interfere unduly with the national marketplace. The word "unduly," to be sure, points to many enduring problems in the federalism of the United States; it will continue to bring many issues to the Supreme Court. Yet the main rationale is clear. It leaves scope for the vitality of all parts of the federal system. Congress through its laws is the main umpire of the system except for the judicially enforced rights that are guaranteed in the national and state constitutions.

These rights are enforced actively by the courts. Outstanding as a protection against the national government are the guarantees of the Fifth Amendment, which among other provisions declares that no person shall "be deprived of life, liberty, or property without due process of law." The Fourteenth Amendment, ratified in 1868, employs the same phrase in restraining state action. The concept of "due process of law," along with other constitutional guarantees, have been applied since mid-century in three momentous fields: the apportionment of members in state and local legislative bodies; the right to vote; and equal access to school systems without segregation.

In these matters the courts are protecting certain of the basic processes that underlie a democratic society. The standard for legislative apportionment popularly called "one man-one vote" is procedural in essence; it does not concern the laws to be passed. So too is equal access to education without the stultifying effects of racial segregation; universal education is a basic feature of democratic societies. Thus it has been consistent for the courts to enforce the constitutional guarantees on these and like matters at the very time when they were ceasing to invalidate congressional and state laws on economic and related subjects, except in preventing state and local action from infringing upon the national controls. The double process in which the courts have withdrawn on one side while advancing on the other is a major feature in the maturing of federalism in the United States.

THE REFLEX OF FEDERALISM UPON PARTY
STRUCTURE AND POLICY

Federalism partly decentralizes the structures of the political parties. Thus in the United States a national party is a congeries of state elements. The federal system, however, has not precluded the existence of national parties and a two-party system (with minor fringes) during most of the country's history. This outcome has been influenced by a balance of forces that has included many things. Probably the presidency—a single office with great powers—has been the strongest institutional factor in bringing about and preserving the two-party system in the face of the size and diversity of the country and the importance of party organization at the state level and below. Another factor has been the prevalence of the single-member district system in electing legislative bodies in contrast to such methods as proportional representation. In addition, not least in the United States, are habits of thought and behavior that are deeper than the structural forms of government and are subtly diffused among the people. These include a fondness for large-scale ways of doing things with a liking also for change but change in unison, accompanied by a practical indifference about fine shadings of doctrine. Whatever the weighting may be among the foregoing and other causes that affect the political system, the outcome is suited for mass choices of a broad nature.

CENTRAL REGULATORY CONTROLS

Mandatory control in certain pervasive areas by the national government is indispensable. The emerging needs for it that are now apparent cannot be met by the incomplete regulation that sufficed earlier in the country's history. Already the nation's power to regulate interstate commerce has been construed in ways that allow Congress to deal comprehensively with certain national issues. Nevertheless, the completeness of the nation's mandatory control will not displace the states. Much of the responsibility can be devolved upon such states as are willing to enact and enforce standards that are at least equal to those imposed by the central government. The indispensable feature is the fullness of the central government's mandatory regulation of things like pollution in its many forms. The essence of the control must be national.

No assurance of a favorable outcome exists apart from awareness, conscience, and the will that is expressed through the political process. It is idle to deny that much which is presently valued must be given up in the choices that lead to desirable ends. Up to a certain point, many options remain open and more will be discovered. For example, remarks Milton Katz of the Harvard Law School, "by taking advantage of this wider range of choices, we can incorporate antipollution controls right into the technological and industrial process itself." He adds: "We can, but will we do so?"

Developments, even in the fields of service, will not all go in the same direction. Old age insurance has been a national system from its beginnings in the thirties. Now it is desirable that social security as a whole be nationalized. This step will relieve the states and localities of a heavy burden. It will get rid of their disparate standards with their unwholesome effects upon interstate migration. In a society that is highly mobile it will over the long run universalize a method that has existed in old age insurance from its beginning. Yet the shift to the nation of the remainder of social security is not a reason against unconditional subsidies to and through the states as a permanent supplement to the restructured system of conditional grants-in-aid.

In the multiplying and widening fields of governmental services the flow to the states and localities of money from the country's tax pool along with ideas nationalized in part from local experience has become a main feature of federalism in the United States. The system of grants-in-aid that once was sporadic and was viewed mainly as a stimulative device is evolving into the country's own version of indirect federal administration. In the field of services it will be increasingly customary for the central government to act through the machinery of the state and local governments, to share its money and its purposes with them, and to depend upon the plenitude of state powers. The growth of these relationships presages a distinctive stage of federalism.

STATE AND LOCAL ROLES IN AN EVOLVING SYSTEM
OF INDIRECT ADMINISTRATION

The United States did well in abandoning the dream of those (most of them opponents of governmental activities generally) who early in the present century were advocating a neat separation of tax sources among the governmental levels. Since that time the national income tax has grown rapidly, and has become the chief pillar of the country's fiscal structure; its yields run ahead of the growth rate of the gross national product. The general property tax is consigned almost wholly to the local governments. It is their main support and is heavily burdened. Sales taxes of many kinds, widely used at state and local levels, are regressive; their use is pardonable, however, in view of the relative general well-being in the American society as a whole. The use by the states of their own forms of personal income taxes, already widespread, is likely to increase. There will be a growing use of the reporting forms and methods of the national income tax. The United States, unlike India, is unlikely wholly to nationalize the income tax. Indeed its use in the form of a payroll tax, so-called, has spread among many municipal governments.

Basically, however, the state and local governments must get an increasing part of their support from the national tax pool. The central government's ability to raise money is superior, with few exceptions, to that of any smaller jurisdiction. Meanwhile, the needs and expenditures of the state and local governments, already high, tend to grow steadily. Some of their outlays actually increase in periods of economic downswings. In such periods it is the national government that can afford to face deficits and to borrow in playing its part in the crucial counter-cyclical role. The resilience of federalism today and in the future lies partly in the flexibility and adaptiveness of these fiscal relationships.

Retaining but Supplementing
the Functional Bridges

Collaboration nationally through the state and local governments will move mostly over what may be called functional bridges. These will survive as a main feature of co-operative federalism. The purposes of national grants-in-aid will broaden, however, with less detail in the central government's prescriptions and more leeway left to the states and localities. Already Congress has merged some of the programs that had taken form under separate laws. The movement toward consolidation is desirable. It is likely, however, to be achieved in stages. Pioneering in the future will appear in new fields with grants-in-aid made available for novel purposes that are well defined and thus will be relatively narrow in their range. Their consolidation will come later. As a whole the broadly cumulative movement will be toward a goal that is desirable in the intergovernmental relations of a modern federal system: a pervasive stimulus with leeway for wide discretion at the lower levels.

The need for collaboration grows. It calls not only for an interlocking with administration in the states and localities but also and increasingly, regardless of future departmental reorganization, for joint action among national agencies. These tendencies were illustrated in the duties given jointly to the departments of the Interior and of Agriculture in cost-sharing with state boards for the conduct of a pilot program called the youth conservation corps.[1]

Most national grants-in-aid will remain categorical, but, as has been said, the categories will broaden. The possibilities were indicated in the President's budget message to Congress in 1971. It recommended that about half of an increased flow of funds from the national tax pool to the states and localities should go under the name of "revenue sharing"

1. Public Law 91-378, 84 Stat. 794, August 13, 1970.

for six broadly defined purposes. These purposes and the recommended amounts in billions of dollars of national aid for the initial year of the system were as follows: urban community development (2 billion); rural community development (1 billion); education (3 billion); manpower training (2 billion); transportation (2.6 billion); and law enforcement (a half billion). It was assumed that the amounts would grow through the years in keeping with the expanding base of the nation's personal income tax. This part of the total system of federal aid to states and localities would be categorical but would be assigned to broader purposes. The crucial questions for the future would include the definitions of these purposes, the formulas and other arrangements for the sharing of the national grants between and among state and local governments, and the methods of accountability.

Unconditional grants as an accompanying feature are debatable. Fortunately, little has been heard in recent years of the idea of supplanting the whole system of conditional grants-in-aid by unconditional grants. As a supplement, however, they are a different matter. In these terms they were broached in the mid-sixties by the then chairman of the Council of Economic Advisers; he repeated the proposal (called the "Heller Plan") after his return to academic life. In 1971 a reformulation of the idea was put before Congress in a presidential message. This proposal for a supplementary system of unconditional grants was strengthened by the fact that the total sum was not to be divided among the states on the basis of population alone. Rather, in line with a theory that had gained support in recent decades, it proposed to take account of the degree to which each state's tax system draws upon that state's taxable resources. "By using a distribution formula which takes their tax effort into account," said the presidential message, "this program would encourage the states to bear a fair share of responsibility. A state which makes a stronger effort to meet its own needs would receive more help from the Federal Government."

The proposal also sought to solve (at least in part) an issue that is troublesome in many forms of grants-in-aid and that is deepened in revenue sharing: the division of a national grant between each state and its local governments. An alternative double answer to this problem was suggested. One alternative was the invitation to each state to negotiate with its local governments in agreeing on a mutually acceptable formula for passing money to the local levels. The other alternative would apply if no such arrangement was agreed upon. The division between the state government and the local units would be on the basis of the relative amounts raised each year by taxation at the respective levels.

A related need is to make sure that the national support (whether conditional or unconditional) does not lessen the willingness of the states and localities to tax themselves in proportion to their resources. Much light has been thrown on this problem by the Advisory Commission on Intergovernmental Relations.[2] Further light will be useful, even crucial, in connection with an increase of the proportion of support of state and local governments from the national tax pool.

Most, if not all, forms of national grants-in-aid should be open to state participation. The universal inclusion of the states, however, is hardly desirable, particularly in the early stages in the development of a new or experimental approach to federalism. The states, which differ in area, population, and taxable wealth (although not in legal powers), vary widely in their current interest and alertness. The reapportionment of state legislative representatives will doubtless make them more uniform in their responsiveness to many problems which bother Congress, which are on the minds of most state governors, and which are an alarming reality for many city mayors. But the effects of these reflexes

2. Advisory Commission on Intergovernmental Relations, *Fiscal Balance in the American Federal System* (Washington, D.C.: U.S. Government Printing Office, 1967, in two volumes), especially pp. 76–87.

come unevenly and slowly. Some differences are inherent; federalism in such a country as the United States is justified for the dateless future in part because these differences exist. At the same time they are among the reasons for not channeling all national grants-in-aid through the state governments. But the option should be open.

A meaningful step in what has been a developing movement was taken in 1971 through passage of the national Intergovernmental Personnel Act.[3] It declares that "effective State and local governmental institutions are essential in the maintenance and development of the Federal system in an increasingly complex and interdependent society," and that therefore "a national interest exists in a high caliber of public service in State and local governments." This interest warrants the national government in providing financial and technical assistance to these governments in strengthening their personnel systems. Such help, says the law, must be given in ways that "encourage innovation and allow for diversity on the part of State and local governments in the design, execution, and management of their own systems of personnel administration." Accordingly, the United States Civil Service Commission is authorized to make grants (running up to 75 per cent) to help in meeting the costs of strengthening personnel administration in the states and localities. Each governor or chief executive authority has primary responsibility for developing the collaborative program at the state level.

Among the conditions is the establishment of merit personnel administrations where appropriate and the improvement of existing systems based on merit principles. A further condition requires "assurance that the making of a Federal Government grant will not result in a reduction in relevant State or local government expenditures or the substitution of Federal funds for State or local funds previously made

3. Public Law 91-648, 84 Stat. 1909, January 5, 1971.

available for these purposes." The objectives include a state-wide personnel system of general or special functional coverage to meet the needs of local governments that are not able to provide sound career services, opportunities for advancement, adequate retirement and leave systems, and other career inducements to well-qualified professional, administrative, and technical personnel.

This lengthy law also provides that the U.S. Civil Service Commission "may join, on a shared-costs basis, with State and local governments in cooperative recruiting and examining activities under such procedures and regulations as may jointly be agreed upon." The statute authorizes aid in the training of personnel as one of its main objectives. The arrangement for mobility of public employees is an interesting feature of the new statute, which provides for the temporary exchange of personnel among the national government, the state and local governments, and institutions of higher education. Provision is made for meeting the expenses of travel and temporary relocation. Especially useful are the provisions that guarantee that the shift in locale will not hurt the individual's retirement and health benefits.

The law as a whole signalizes a major step toward the concerted use of public personnel in the United States. But it is part of a secular growth. Thus it should be noted that between the beginning of 1969, when the Civil Service Commission was first authorized to provide reimbursable training to the personnel of state and local governments, and the middle of the following year the commission had trained over four thousand state and local employees, with the number increasing each month. Moreover, on the recruiting side there were already the beginnings of procedures that amounted to a joint announcement, examination, and referral process for certain types of positions. In all these domains useful pioneering had been going on for three decades under the office of state merit systems in the Department of Health, Education, and Welfare.

The Role of Local Units of General Government
A desirable emphasis in national grants-in-aid at the local level is a growing stress upon units of general government. But local boundaries constitute a serious problem. They are often unfair to many groups in the form in which they exist. Indeed, their rigidity has increased in recent decades, in part to bulwark the exclusionary policies of the suburban municipalities. It is time for the revision of many boundaries. The problem is a state and local matter but the national government has some leverage through national grants-in-aid or other support, as in housing. Looking to the future, it is timely to consider how the long-run geography of local government can be improved without abandoning the fundamentals of self-government.

The objectives at stake can make terms, although not easily, with the mounting clamor for smaller and more manageable urban governments. A middle ground for progress in such a country as the United States, especially while its population continues to grow, will be the building of new cities of moderate size with work near to where people live. Other countries have shown the promising possibilities if not fully satisfactory solutions.[4] Models are appearing in the United States. Here is a task for the remainder of the present century. But such developments are not a substitute for the incipient attempts to find ways of decentralizing parts of the process by which people can share more actively in helping to administer many programs within the large cities that now exist.

A promising sign is the invitation to local planning extended in recent federal aid laws. The Intergovernmental Cooperation Act of 1968, a modest landmark in the progress toward a still more workable federalism in a modern nation, is sound in providing that "To the maximum extent pos-

---

4. Frank Schaffer, *The New Town Story* (London: Macgibbon and Kee, 1970).

sible, consistent with national objectives, all Federal aid for development purposes shall be consistent with and further the objectives of State, regional, and local comprehensive planning."[5] A kindred spirit is shown by the Soil Conservation Society of America in its national policy for land use, which asks "that federal grants and programs be administered in conformity with land use plans developed by local governments and not deviate from them without valid reasons that clearly establish justification."[6]

The United States has much to learn from other federations but also has something to teach. Not least of the lessons will be the harmonious interlocking among the levels of planning. James L. Sundquist, cited in earlier pages for his first-hand inquiries and for his insight, writes about the need to perfect planning and coordinating machinery in the thousands of communities that comprise the country. "Then, *as the machinery begins to measure up to its promise and gains in competence,*" he writes (the italics are his own), "the conscious policy of the federal government as a whole—and, hopefully, the state governments as well—should be *to defer increasingly to local judgments.*"[7] This reflects a sound view. But sound too is the verdict that follows on the next page: "Much is lost, obviously, if the federal government fails to exert leadership."

INTERLEVEL AGREEMENTS AMONG ADMINISTRATORS

The preceding summary has spoken of the widening of federal aid into what amounts to a new sort of indirect administration in the federal system, especially in the growing fields

---

5. Public Law 90-577, 82 Stat. 1098, Section 401 (c), October 16, 1968.
6. *Journal of Soil and Water Conservation*, XXV, No. 2 (March-April 1970), 72.
7. James L. Sundquist with the collaboration of David W. Davis, *Making Federalism Work: A Study of Program Coordination at the Community Level* (Washington, D.C.: The Brookings Institution, 1969), p. 250.

of service where compulsory controls are incidental rather than primary. This setting has led to comment on some aspects of the future of local government. At this point it will be useful to note that the interlevel developments already in progress will not remove the need for a wide array of agreements between various national agencies and their counterparts in particular states. Such agreements came with the beginnings of federalism in the United States, although they were so piecemeal and informal that they were little noted. Yet, though not peculiar to federalism, they have always contributed to the vitality of federal government. These understandings are indispensable wherever parts or phases of a common function are conducted by governments at different levels. Federalism with its divisions sharpens the need.

An uncounted number and range of understandings exist among national and state and local administrators, and they are multiplying. The word "agreement" is the usual term by which they are described, though sometimes, still more modestly, they are called memoranda of understanding. Occasionally they are labeled contracts. Even when in contract form, these working relations seldom if ever get into the courts. They are prompted and propelled by a shared concern. Some of them doubtless would profit by the clarification and firmness that courts might provide. Perhaps it has been enough to resort occasionally to a ruling by the attorney general of the state or of the national government. Where the animating motive is the mutual advantage of a working relation, the sanctions would not often be found in judicial decisions. A kind of control exists in the possibility of withdrawal by a dissatisfied participant. In many kinds of administrative work the routines of joint activity become so habitual that the original written document is almost forgotten. The observer may be disappointed but he is not surprised when (as sometimes happens) the original agreement itself cannot be found. Even when the basic arrangement not only is written but is kept carefully on file, the joint operations tend to evolve in practice through correspondence and face-to-face dealings.

Collaboration on the basis of signed agreements is more than an expedient for overcoming the inconveniences arising from the division of power in federal systems. This fact is shown not only in the practices of unitary forms of government but also in the use of written agreements among departments and bureaus within one level. They abound within the national government of the United States where, desirable as will be the recurrent restructuring of its departments, much will be handled through interagency agreements. This fact does not belittle the value of personal relations and acquaintanceships, which are part of the essence of the interlevel dealings that are accented by federalism. These personal ties do not, of course, make clarity and precision less important. These traits are especially crucial where sizable sums of money are involved or where equipment is shared or loaned. The practice of federalism is full of working relationships that involve a definition of duties as part of a cooperative responsibility. It profits by explicitness at key points. A signed agreement, whether called a contract or merely a memorandum of understanding, is often indispensable.

Such signed understandings have two special virtues. On the one hand they are flexible, each suiting a particular purpose. On the other hand, since the basis is mutual advantage, the possibility of refusal or withdrawal constantly injects the healthy corrective of criticism. Looking to the future, the interlevel agreements on particular matters are causeways that will carry still heavier loads. Despite what has been said, therefore, future agreements will profit by more formality, exactness, and the possibilities sometimes for judicial interpretation and enforcement. It has been noted that in the different but related field of interstate compacts the availability of the courts has helped on occasion to interpret and lend weight to the commitments. The usefulness of judicial action in exceptional circumstances is not refuted by the Supreme Court's advice on one occasion, as noted in the preceding chapter, that the issue at hand might better be dealt with by an agreement than by action in the courts.

IMPROVING THE NATION'S MACHINERY: REGIONAL AND CENTRAL COORDINATION

A standard set of intermediate administrative regions can aid in harmonizing the policies of different national agencies that have dealings with the states and localities. Their contact in such regions can help in adjusting the downward projection of their separate programs. It can also assist in bringing the contiguous states closer together. These possibilities are becoming realities in the ten standard, multipurpose regions that have been recently formed by the national government. Each is a combination of whole states, thus making easier consultative relations with the state governments. The goal for each region is a common headquarters for the regional heads of the national departments. The city where these shared headquarters are located becomes a kind of administrative capital for the area.

A Shared System of Regional Headquarters

The standardizing of a regional structure for numerous national departments and agencies is not easily arranged. Each governmental program is likely to have distinctive needs that seem to point to a unique supervisory area. Thus the inspection system that is part of grain standardization under a congressional law is likely to be interested in developing the kind of shoestring districts that extend from the main points of assembly along the lines of shipment to the chief produce markets. The officials in charge of immigration control are apt to prefer to organize their administrative districts along the country's borders in the form of narrow regions that cross many states. Even where the seeming needs are not so special, each national bureau or agency has tended to create a subnational structure of its own.

The patterns in the past varied among and even within the national departments. Different areal patterns sometimes developed under the same bureau or division. Many of the reasons for these diversities were sound in themselves, resting as they did on the specifically functional nature of the work to be done. Sometimes this claim cannot be denied. Mostly, so far as it is valid, it can be met through the use of supervisory areas below the level of the standard regions. The case for the latter gathered strength by the wish to decentralize many of the departmental decisions along with the desire to have more consistency among the separate programs. Early in the seventies the movement took form at last in the ten shared regions.

Each region has a council that brings together the top representatives in the area of a number of national agencies. At the start of the scheme they came from the departments of Health, Education and Welfare, Housing and Urban Development, and Transportation, from the manpower administration in the Labor Department, and from the Office of Economic Opportunity. It was customary for the regional representatives of other bodies, including the Commerce Department, the General Services Administration, and the Civil Service Commission, to join on an ad hoc basis. Each council chooses its own chairman, with rotation at regular intervals. The details of membership and organization are not important; they will shift through time. The purpose and the promise are more durable.

Three objectives were given to the councils in 1970. One purpose is to identify any conflicting points of agency policy or operating procedures that hamper the effectiveness of assistance by the national government to the state, localities, and individuals. A second objective is to devise the mutually consistent sorts of agency actions that will make the national programs more effective. The third main purpose is to aid each regional head of a national program in doing the things that will strengthen coordination among programs and that will help in monitoring them and in evaluating how they are implemented. Broadly, the council in each of the ten regions is seen as a focus for relations with the state and local governments.

This regional machinery can help in bettering the concert among a number of national programs. In itself, the scheme did not guarantee that there would be more scope for state and local decisions within the nationally aided programs. Nevertheless, the common regional headquarters do help to bring more consistency among the national objectives at the point where they impinge upon the state and local governments. Much will depend on how the national programs are couched. The question will involve many issues about the nature and extent of the nation's responsibility for the collaborative undertakings that it helps to finance.

Concert at the Center

A budget circular, attended by a revised set of regulations, sought to enlarge upon the President's duty under the law in establishing rules for "the formulation, evaluation, and review of Federal programs and projects having a significant impact on area and community development." It said that the chief executives of state and local government would be given a reasonable opportunity to comment on major proposed regulations, standards, procedures, and guidelines that were likely to have a significant effect on state and local governments. The need for such consultation in advance was stressed in a revised circular to the heads of executive departments and agencies early in 1971.

In the national capitol much can be done through liaison among the departments and agencies. Part of the hope for coordination lies within the Executive Office of the President. A start has been made in devising machinery for the harmonizing of domestic purposes and programs. The exact structure and its place in the executive office will vary over time. In 1969, departing slightly from an earlier arrangement, a staff called the Office of Intergovernmental Relations with a director was formed under an executive order to "serve as the clearinghouse for the prompt handling of Federal-State-local problems brought to the attention of the President or Vice President by executive and legislative officers of state and local governments." Each governmental agency was asked to designate an official with broad general experience as a point of contact in connection with interlevel activities.

CONCLUSION

Basically, however, before administration begins, separate laws advance one by one in a progress that inherently is uneven. The potential inconsistencies can be avoided only in part. This fact increases the need for enough decentralization under each law to allow scope for coordination regionally not only of matters that are handled mainly through the state and local governments but also of the activities that are carried out directly by the national government.

Looking into a future already at hand, it was wisely said by a congressional report in 1970: "There is no acceptable justification for a policy that controls only those sources that are easily and conveniently controlled." Many things besides preservation of the environment will involve profound choices in the coming decades and will call for "a commitment to make sacrifices, to spend money, and to give up some technological comforts and luxuries."

Index